INVEST WITH MIND:
THE TEMPERAMENT FOR SUCCESSFUL RETIREMENT

INVEST WITH MIND:
THE TEMPERAMENT FOR SUCCESSFUL RETIREMENT

Smarter Strategies, Resilient Portfolios,
and Peace of Mind for Life

DOV MARSHALL
CFP, CLU, CIM, PORTFOLIO MANAGER

CERTIFIED

(H)

WRITTEN
BY HUMAN

DISCLAIMER

The views, opinions, and positions expressed in this book are solely those of the author in the author's personal capacity and do not necessarily reflect the views, opinions, positions, or policies of Aligned Capital Partners Inc., its affiliates, directors, officers, employees, or agents (collectively, "ACPI"). Any references to ACPI are for identification purposes only. This publication is not sponsored, endorsed, approved, or reviewed by ACPI. No statement in this book should be construed as an official statement, commitment, or representation of ACPI. This book is for educational and informational purposes only and does not constitute investment, legal, tax, accounting, or other professional advice, or a solicitation, recommendation, or offer to buy or sell any security or financial instrument. The information is general in nature and may not be appropriate for any particular investor. Readers should consult their own qualified advisors before making any financial decisions. Nothing in this publication establishes a fiduciary relationship between the author and any reader, nor does it create an advisory-client relationship with ACPI. Past performance is not indicative of future results. All investments involve risk, including the possible loss of principal.

CONTENTS

FROM MANUELLE HASENFELD REGARDING THE PUBLISHING OF THIS BOOK

I was pleased to hear about Dov's book INVEST WITH MIND: THE TEMPERAMENT FOR SUCCESSFUL RETIREMENT. Working closely with Dov over the last six years, I have seen firsthand how his advice to clients and his approach to investing is superb and grounded in both wisdom and practicality. His ability to simplify complex ideas while keeping clients focused on long-term goals, his analytical skill on the markets, combined with his client-centric approach to portfolio construction, is unique in this industry.

With more than forty years of my own experience in the investment field, I can confidently say that Dov stands out for his integrity, clarity of thought, and genuine care for the people he serves. This book reflects those very qualities—it's not just about numbers, but about cultivating the mindset needed to navigate your specific financial situation to achieve lasting peace of mind in retirement.

I am proud to call Dov a colleague and a friend, and I believe readers will find in this book the same wisdom, integrity, and steady guidance that he has brought to many clients over the years.

Manuelle Hasenfeld, Investment Advisor of four decades

INTRODUCTION

"Your money or your life?--I'm thinking it over."

–Jack Benny

Money—just the word—carries incredible power. For some, it symbolizes freedom and confidence, a tool for achieving dreams and securing the future. For others, it's a source of confusion, stress, or even destructive behavior.

Consider the term *affluenza*—a word coined to describe the psychological challenges faced by those born into extreme wealth. It underscores the darker side of abundance: when money lacks purpose and substance, it can lead to irrational choices and personal turmoil. The same force that can uplift and empower can also drag one into the depths of poor decisions if left unchecked.

As an investment advisor and portfolio manager, I've seen both sides of money's impact. My role gives me a front-row seat to the irrational behaviors of markets and the complex, deeply personal ways people interact with their wealth. I don't just analyze investments or study market trends—I work directly with people to understand their unique fears, goals, and dreams regarding money.

This dual perspective sets me apart. While many financial professionals either focus solely on the mechanics of the market or exclusively on client relationships, I've chosen to bridge the gap. By combining rigorous investment research with a deep understanding of client psychology, I've developed a unique approach: aligning investment strategies with individual values, ambitions, and emotions.

The Emotional Side of Wealth

No matter where you are on your financial journey—whether you've already amassed millions or are just starting out—money is more than numbers on a balance sheet. It's tied to our deepest emotions, especially fear and greed, which are the two most significant obstacles to financial success.

Fear keeps people frozen. It leads them to park their money in low-interest savings accounts, missing out on the potential for long-term growth because they're terrified of losing what they've worked so hard to save. On the other hand, greed pushes people to take unnecessary risks—chasing quick returns, throwing all their savings into speculative ventures, and often losing it all in the process.

Statistics reveal these patterns clearly:

- The majority of individual investors underperform the market because they make emotional, short-sighted decisions.
- Many fail to invest altogether, paralyzed by fear and a lack of knowledge.

This book is designed to break those cycles. It offers a new mindset and a practical roadmap to help you achieve peace of mind with your wealth while building a sustainable and prosperous financial future.

What You'll Learn

In these pages, you'll discover a comprehensive approach to investing that integrates rational strategies with emotional balance. You'll gain insights into:

- **Diversification Done Right**: How to build a portfolio that spreads risk effectively while positioning you for growth.

- **Understanding Different Investment Types**: From stocks and bonds to alternative assets and options, we'll explore how these elements work together in a cohesive investment plan.

- **Managing Emotions**: Practical tools to keep fear and greed from sabotaging your financial decisions.

- **Developing a Peaceful Money Mindset**: Strategies to help you approach wealth with confidence and clarity, no matter the market conditions.

This book isn't about quick fixes or gimmicks. It's about helping you cultivate a relationship with money that is grounded, informed, and empowering. Whether you're climbing the financial ladder or preserving the wealth you've already built, you'll find actionable advice and thought-provoking ideas to guide you toward your goals.

A Journey Toward Financial Confidence

The road to financial success isn't just about numbers—it's about understanding yourself and making choices aligned with your values. This book is your companion on that journey. It's a seamless tapestry of practical solutions and timeless wisdom woven together to help you achieve both financial growth and inner peace.

Let's begin this journey together. With the right tools, mindset, and strategies, you can create a future where money becomes a source of stability, joy, and fulfillment—not fear or frustration.

Why Write a Book?

Why would I write a book and share all my insights—essentially giving away my "secrets"—for free or at such a modest price? It's a question some may ask, especially those who approach life with a scarcity mindset. This perspective leads people to believe that sharing knowledge or ideas means losing out, as though someone else's gain automatically diminishes their own.

I don't subscribe to that belief. I see things quite differently.

I embrace an abundance mindset. When we help others, we enrich not only their lives but also our own. Money and success are not zero-sum games. When one person achieves financial growth or stability, it doesn't mean someone else must lose. On the contrary, the positive effects ripple outward, uplifting entire communities and fostering a cycle of shared prosperity.

Sharing the lessons I've learned is about multiplying the good that can come from it. These insights are the result of years of hands-on experience in the markets and close interactions with clients. They've been honed through hard work, mistakes, and breakthroughs. I've seen firsthand how these principles can transform financial lives, and I believe they're meant to be shared.

The Gift of Knowledge

Sharing knowledge is like giving a gift. Just as charity fulfills the purpose of wealth, sharing these ideas fulfills the purpose of the experiences and lessons I've been fortunate enough to gain. When you give, whether it's money, time, or wisdom, you're not just benefiting the recipient—you're living out the true purpose of what you've been given.

This book is my way of giving forward. It's a tool to help others navigate the complexities of money and investing with clarity and confidence. It's a way to multiply the impact of what I've learned so others can use these principles to create success in their own lives.

By helping others achieve financial peace of mind, we contribute to a world where more people can thrive. And when more people thrive, everyone benefits.

As you read through the pages of this book, my hope is that it will equip you with the tools, insights, and mindset to create true abundance in your life. Not just material wealth but a more profound, meaningful abundance—one rooted in personal fulfillment, clarity, and purpose.

Abundance isn't just about the numbers on a balance sheet or the size of an investment portfolio. It's about achieving growth in every dimension of life—your finances, your mindset, and your sense of purpose within our shared world. True abundance is about crafting a life where peace of mind and prosperity coexist, empowering you to make confident, rational decisions that align with your deepest values and goals. Living with abundance is about living a life of continuous growth that surpasses your current expectations and enriches your life and the lives of those around you.

If you have questions, thoughts, or reflections as you journey through this book, I would genuinely love to hear from you. Your feedback is invaluable to me, and it brings me great joy to connect with readers who are on their own unique paths toward financial and personal success. Please don't hesitate to reach out—I'm here to listen, learn, and continue this conversation with you.

Thank you for allowing me to share these ideas with you.

Blessings for your continued growth, abundance, and success!

CHAPTER #1

Frozen Like a Deer
in the Headlights

"The greatest risk is the risk of riskless living."

– Stephen R. Covey

The Psychology of Fear and Investment Paralysis

You've just inherited $2 million, an amount most people dream of but never see. It's sitting in a savings account, and there's no denying that having this kind of money should bring you a sense of freedom, security, and excitement. Instead, it leaves you feeling paralyzed. Like a deer caught in the headlights, you can't move— too afraid to make a wrong decision that could ruin everything.

On one hand, you know leaving it in a savings account isn't the best move. The returns are meager, inflation chips away at its value over time, and deep down, you know there's more that could be done with it. On the other hand, investing feels like stepping into a jungle, and you're petrified of what could go wrong.

Stories of people losing fortunes flood your mind—nightmares of stocks crashing, real estate bubbles bursting, and cryptocurrency scandals that wipe out entire portfolios. You've seen the headlines: "Investors Lose Millions Overnight," "Markets Plummet," "Recession Fears Spark Panic."

If that wasn't enough, you're bombarded daily with conflicting information: experts on TV predicting market corrections, influencers hyping the next big thing, and financial websites forecasting the next downturn. It's a whirlwind of noise, and amidst it all, one emotion reigns supreme—fear.

Why does your stomach knot whenever you think about making an investment? Why do you immediately second-guess yourself? The answer lies deep within human psychology.

Fear is one of the most powerful emotions, and when it comes to money, it can become magnified. For many, the idea of losing even a portion of their savings feels catastrophic. Loss aversion, a term popularized by behavioral economists, describes how people feel the pain of loss much more powerfully than the pleasure of an equivalent gain. Losing $100 feels worse than gaining $100 feels good. This imbalance causes people to be overly cautious, focusing more on avoiding losses than on achieving gains.

Daniel Kahneman and Amos Tversky originally coined the term "loss aversion" in 1979.

That fear results in a condition known as "investment paralysis." This psychological state arises when fear overtakes rational decision-making, causing you to refrain from taking any action.

Like a deer caught in headlights, you become paralyzed, unable to move in any direction. You convince yourself, "I'll wait until things feel more certain."

You likely have worked hard to earn your nest egg and are rightfully afraid of it dwindling away due to bad investment choices. Haven't we all heard of those successful people who lose a large chunk of their wealth in one bad venture? You may have gotten burned in bad investment ventures in the past. You may be "traumatized" from past losses. You may be thinking, "Better a bird in the hand than two in the bush. Why take any risk?"

You've picked up the right book. This book will help you move forward successfully. It will help you understand the risks and how to avoid them. It will be your road map, directing you on how to avoid the potholes around the city. As you pursue successfully investing your retirement portfolio, keep this book on hand as a reference guide.

The Trap of Information Overload

Compounding the problem is the modern-day curse of information overload. Anyone with a smartphone has access to unlimited financial data, but more information isn't always better. In fact, it often leads to more significant confusion.

Studies have shown that when people are presented with too much information, their decision-making process suffers. You might be trying to read every article, listen to every podcast, and follow every market analyst in an attempt to "get it right," but all this does is create more doubt.

Paralysis by analysis is the result. Instead of clarifying the picture, all this information creates a fog. One moment, you think investing in stocks makes sense because they have historically provided good returns. The next moment, you read an article about the potential for a looming recession, and suddenly, you're convinced that the stock market is a house of cards. The pendulum swings back and forth, and you're left immobilized.

Yes, you need to do your due diligence. And take your time to get the story right about any prospective investment. Read up on the latest news about the topic and think it through till you have clarity. But you need to know what information is helpful and what information is not. Not every market pundit or stock guru shares information that is relevant to you. They may say, "Buy XYZ stock now," but the pundit/guru only plans to invest short-term while you are a long-term investor. I see this with clients all the time. A client will say, "This or that online site rates XYZ stock a C, shouldn't we sell it?" I explain that the site ratings are focused on the next one to three months, while we are focused on the long-term. Our advantage being investors looking out several years is that we can take advantage of others selling down a stock due to short-term noise and news. When I choose a stock company, I'm looking at the long-term projected growth. While I don't ignore the short term, I usually file the noise away in the noise file.

The Emotional Rollercoaster of Risk

What's at the heart of your hesitation around investments?

It's the emotional relationship you have with risk. For some, risk is exciting—a thrill-seeking venture where the potential for reward is worth the uncertainty. But for many, risk is terrifying. It's not just about numbers; it's about what those numbers represent—your security, your future, your dreams, and your prestige.

The fear of losing what you already have often outweighs the potential joy of gaining more. This isn't just true for large sums of money, like the $2 million you may have earned or inherited. It happens to investors at every level. Beginners and seasoned professionals alike grapple with the emotional volatility that comes with investing.

Markets fluctuate. Investments go up and down, and no matter how much data you analyze, there's always a degree of unpredictability. That unpredictability triggers fear, anxiety, and even panic. You might hear stories about people who stayed in the market during a downturn and eventually reaped huge rewards, but it's far more challenging to sit through those dips when your money is on the line.

Here is where effective portfolio allocation proves invaluable. We will explore in depth the strategies for selecting various investment classes or diverse baskets of assets that respond differently during economic shocks.

The Danger of Emotional Decision-Making

So, you've been hearing and reading about the latest hot investment and feel convinced and ready to dive in?

Hold on a moment. One of the biggest risks in investing is letting emotions influence your choices. In times of fear, you might quickly gravitate towards what feels safe, like keeping all your funds in cash. On the other hand, when the market is thriving, you may encounter a fear of missing out, which could push you into high-risk investments without weighing the long-term effects.

This emotional cycle can cause you to buy high and sell low—the opposite of what makes a successful investor. Behavioral economists call this "herding"—following the crowd rather than making rational, informed decisions. You might be tempted to jump into the latest trend, whether it's tech stocks, cryptocurrency, or real estate, because it seems like "everyone else is doing it."

However, successful investing often involves going against the grain after thorough analysis. It requires the discipline to stick to a strategy even when your emotions are screaming at you to do the opposite.

Several years ago, I worked in an office with a few other investment advisors. Every day for months, discussions among these advisors and their clients revolved around an exciting new trend: cannabis stocks. What a rollercoaster ride they experienced! I never bought into the hype; in fact, I never invested a penny in that sector. Do I regret not making money on the way up? A resounding no.

"But why?" you may ask.

I don't want my clients exposed to that risk. I focus on sound fundamentals and ignore all the hype. For this reason, I have yet to invest in Crypto.

Here's a chart depicting a cannabis stock that soared dramatically for several years before experiencing a sharp decline shortly after. This rollercoaster was driven by hype all along.

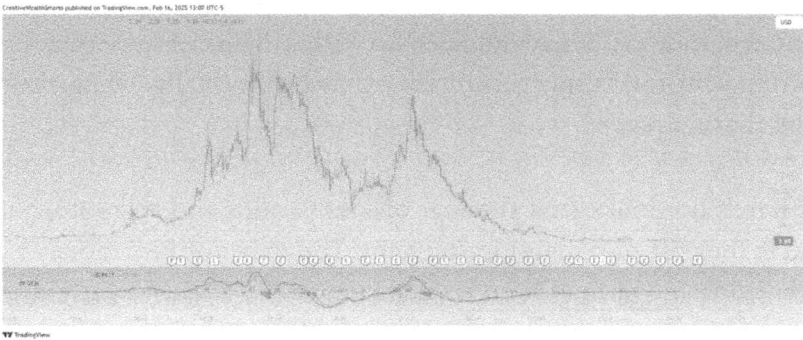

The Trade-off Between Safety and Potential Growth

Maybe you've heard stories from friends or family, about an aunt who invested her inheritance in a hot stock tip or risky real estate venture, only to watch it all evaporate. Stories like these reinforce the idea that investing is a gamble and avoiding the market altogether is safer. This might lead you to consider Guaranteed Investment Certificates (GICs), which offer the security of knowing that your principal investment is protected, even though the returns are minimal.

GICs are attractive, particularly for those who are risk-averse and value safety. They offer a guaranteed return without risking your capital, which brings peace of mind. Yet, this feeling of security has a price—opportunity cost. By remaining in the safe haven of guaranteed returns, are you prepared to miss out on the potential for greater financial growth and, in the end, personal prosperity?

In investing, opportunity cost signifies the potential profits you forfeit by opting for safer, lower-return investments, such as GICs, instead of more volatile, higher-return assets like stocks or real estate. Although GICs can safeguard your capital, the modest interest they yield may not keep up with inflation. Consequently, while your funds stay secure, they may be gradually losing their purchasing power.

There's no doubt that the fear of loss is valid and accurate, but so is the cost of remaining stagnant. You may not lose money by choosing the path of least resistance, but you could be forfeiting the opportunity to secure a better financial future. Just as personal growth arises from facing challenges, economic growth often results from calculated and informed risks. It's not about being reckless; it's about finding a balance between safety and opportunity, between security and growth.

By avoiding risk, you may also be missing out on personal growth. Investing isn't merely about expanding your wealth; it's about developing the skills and mindset necessary to handle uncertainty and make informed decisions. The discomfort of stepping outside your comfort zone can lead to valuable lessons in finance and life. After all, personal growth often arises from facing challenges and taking calculated risks.

Cognitive Bias

Investors often encounter various mental and emotional biases that can lead to irrational decision-making, much like the well-known phenomenon of loss aversion. For instance, some investors might prematurely sell their winning positions, missing out on further gains, while simultaneously clinging to losing investments for too long, hoping to break even. This combination of behaviors can significantly impact their overall investment performance.

A disciplined investment strategy is essential for achieving long-term success. This discipline must be based on thorough research, enabling investors to make informed decisions anchored in data and analysis rather than emotions or unfounded beliefs. By utilizing our analytical skills, we can greatly minimize the impact of cognitive biases that frequently lead to poor investment choices. These biases can cloud our judgment and drive us to react impulsively to market trends, but by prioritizing rigorous research and analysis, we are better positioned to maintain our course and make sound investment decisions. Thus, a solid research foundation not only improves decision-making but also serves as a buffer against the risks posed by cognitive biases.

Conclusion

It's common to feel paralyzed when it comes to investing, particularly with a large amount of money at stake. Various cognitive biases can impede the average investor's success.

By taking deliberate, informed steps, you can turn your multi-million-dollar nest egg of savings into a source of long-term security and growth. The key is to break free from paralysis, embrace manageable and calculated risks, and let strategy, rather than emotion, drive your decisions.

As you will learn in the coming chapters, you can do this easily with the right mindset.

CHAPTER 2

The Correct Investment Mindset

"The market is a pendulum that forever swings between unsustainable optimism (which makes stocks too expensive) and unjustified pessimism (which makes them too cheap). The intelligent investor is a realist who sells to optimists and buys from pessimists."

– Benjamin Graham, The Intelligent Investor

In my practice, I work with a diverse range of clients, including those at opposite ends of the spectrum. Some reach out in distress whenever the news reports something negative, despite enjoying steady, quality returns year after year.

Conversely, others are always eager to take advantage of the latest trends, wanting to purchase stocks that have already surged significantly.

Both of these behaviors can be problematic, and I strive to help them adopt a calmer and more consistent approach.

A Primed Mind

Your mindset about investing and wealth can be primed, optimized, and fine-tuned for success. Just like any athlete must be in the right mental state to jump, sprint, and excel in their sport, the same principle applies to investing. The mental preparation that comes before financial decisions is often underestimated. Even the best strategies can falter without sharp focus and the right mindset.

I'm always striving to refine my investment mindset and perspective. Our brains are like pencils—they need regular sharpening to stay effective. Without that care, they can become dull over time.

A key mental shift is taking a closer look at the thoughts and feelings that might be blocking your path to investment success. What emotions might be holding you back?

Have you ever found yourself acting out of fear, anxiety, or worry about missing out (FOMO)? Our emotions can be powerful influencers; if we don't manage them, they might throw even the most disciplined investor off course. Embracing successful investing means recognizing these feelings and transforming fear and panic into confidence through rational, calm analysis and a long-term perspective vision.

Emotional Barriers to Success

A common roadblock for many investors is panic during short-term market volatility. Many people get caught up in short-term fluctuations and fail to understand that this volatility is often part of a long-term investment strategy. The stock market naturally fluctuates. The key is maintaining a steady focus on long-term goals, even when the market temporarily dips.

When you've done sufficient research on an investment and are confident in its long-term potential, you must remind yourself that market fluctuations are temporary. You've invested in a company with sound fundamentals—strong earnings, a solid balance sheet, and long-term growth potential. When the market inevitably takes a roller-coaster ride, don't let the short-term drops derail your long-term vision.

Consider this: investing in the stock market is akin to committing to a long-term journey. You understand there will be bumps along the way. However, if you've properly diversified your portfolio and allocated a portion of your assets that you're comfortable with, you won't panic when those bumps occur. By ensuring you aren't overextended financially, you can sit back and observe market fluctuations from a place of calm, knowing they are part of the journey.

Effective portfolio construction is paramount to achieving financial stability and growth. As we will explore in detail, a well-structured portfolio should encompass a diverse array of assets, each with distinct characteristics that significantly mitigate market risk and volatility. This diversity ensures that the potential short-term negative performance of one holding does not significantly influence the portfolio as a whole, providing a buffer against market fluctuations. Furthermore, it is crucial to allocate funds thoughtfully; no single investment should constitute an amount greater than what you are entirely comfortable managing. Each investment decision should be made with careful consideration of the potential future directions that each asset may take, allowing for a balanced approach to risk and reward.

Short-Term vs. Long-Term Thinking

One of the most common mindset errors is confusing short-term investing with long-term investing. While they both involve buying assets, they are fundamentally different in terms of strategy and mindset. A short-term investor might focus on rapid gains from market trends, attempting to "time the market" by buying low and selling high in a short span. This approach can be lucrative, but it often involves much higher risk, emotional volatility, and stress.

The long-term investor doesn't sell at the first sign of a downturn; instead, they ride out the storm, knowing that fluctuations are part of the market's natural cycle.

Long-term investing, by contrast, is about patience, research, and a steady approach. It's about understanding that the true value of a company may take years to unfold. Here, the emphasis isn't on short-term market trends but rather on the gradual increase in value of assets over time. The long-term investor doesn't sell at the first sign of a downturn; instead, they ride out the storm, knowing that fluctuations are part of the market's natural cycle.

Investors need to acknowledge that short-term volatility doesn't always indicate a fundamental flaw in the company they've invested in. Instead, fluctuations can be the result of various external factors—political events, market sentiment, and economic shifts—that may have little to do with the company's long-term potential. Staying focused on your long-term goals prevents knee-jerk reactions that could harm your portfolio's growth.

Mindset Blocks and Financial History

Another essential aspect of developing the correct investment mindset involves looking at your past. What stories and beliefs about money did you internalize during your childhood? Early experiences with money often shape how we view investments, risk, and success later in life. If you grew up in a family where money was scarce or the conversation around finances was negative, those fears may still subconsciously guide your decisions today.

Similarly, your past investment experiences—successes and failures—can influence how you approach future opportunities. For example, if you've lost money in a previous investment, you may hesitate to take risks, even when faced with a sound opportunity. Conversely, if you've had quick wins, you may be inclined to chase after fast returns, forgetting the importance of patience and prudence in long-term investing.

The key to overcoming these mindset blocks is self-awareness. Take time to reflect on your personal relationship with money. Are you motivated by fear, anxiety, or greed? Do you find yourself paralyzed by indecision or, conversely, making impulsive decisions without proper analysis? By understanding your mental triggers and biases, you can begin to reframe your thinking, empowering yourself to make better, more informed choices.

Leveraging Strengths and Addressing Weaknesses

Just as athletes train to develop their strengths and overcome their weaknesses, investors must do the same. Take stock of your natural tendencies. Are you someone who is opportunistic and ready to act when the right moment arises, or do you tend to be cautious, only making a move when absolutely necessary?

Both tendencies have their strengths and weaknesses. An opportunistic mindset can lead to bold, successful investments, but it may also lead to impulsive decisions driven by emotion rather than logic. On the other hand, a more cautious approach may prevent you from capitalizing on lucrative opportunities if you are overly conservative.

The key to mastering your investment mindset is to leverage your strengths while managing your weaknesses. If you are prone to impulsivity, impose a rule that you must always take 24 hours to review an investment opportunity before making a decision. This will give you time to step back from the initial excitement and assess the situation rationally. If you are overly cautious, set specific financial goals with deadlines that force you to take action and seize opportunities that align with your strategy.

What's Wrong with Short-Term Investing?

To be clear, there's absolutely nothing wrong with short-term investing; it's just a different set of required temperament, skills, and supervision. Short-term investing is an active strategy (in contrast to passive) and can be quite profitable if the right disciplines are implemented.

Later, I will dedicate a section to maximizing the potential of this strategy.

In my practice, I see how clients struggle when these two distinct strategies are conflated. When you invest for the long term, the short-term fluctuations are just noise and best ignored. If you've put money into a long-term holding but grow anxious, doubting your decision every month as you check your statements amid market pullbacks, you may feel pressured to abandon your investment.

This anxiety can lead to poor decision-making. For example, you might sell your long-term investment prematurely, incurring losses and missing potential future gains. Moreover, by failing to stick to the long-term strategy, you might chase short-term gains, which often contribute to volatile investments and result in unfavorable outcomes. Understanding the distinct objectives and timelines of each strategy is crucial to avoid these pitfalls and ensure a well-rounded investment approach.

"Activity is the enemy of investment returns."
– Warren Buffett

"The single greatest edge an investor can have is a long-term orientation."

– Seth Klarman

"Time is your Friend, Impulse is your Enemy."

– John Bogle

Conclusion: Building a Mindset for Success

Developing the correct investment mindset requires self-awareness, emotional control, and a clear long-term vision. It's about recognizing the role that emotions like fear and greed play in investment decisions and learning to replace them with logic, research, and patience.

Success in investing isn't just about picking the right stocks, bonds or funds, or having the most sophisticated financial tools. It's about having the mental fortitude to stay the course, even when the market throws you off balance. By fine-tuning your mindset, embracing long-term thinking, and managing your emotional responses, you'll set yourself up for lasting success.

CHAPTER 3

Opportunity Cost in Investing

"Intelligent people make decisions based on opportunity costs."

— Charlie Munger

Opportunity Cost

Opportunity cost is one of the most powerful concepts in investing. It is the value of what you forgo by choosing one investment over another. In the context of retirement investing, opportunity cost is often the difference between a portfolio that grows exponentially and one that lags due to suboptimal decisions. Understanding this principle can mean the difference between a comfortable retirement and merely getting by.

Compounding and Opportunity Cost

One of the simplest yet most profound illustrations of opportunity cost is through compounding returns. If left unchecked, cognitive biases that lead to conservative or poor investment choices can significantly limit your portfolio's growth potential. Over a 30-year horizon, the difference between a 10% annual return and a 4% annual return can result in either 17.4X or just 3.2X growth in your nest egg.

Let's break this down.

Take a financial calculator, or go online to this <u>finance calculator</u>[1] to see the math behind the magic of compounding. Here's how it works. We want to calculate the future value (FV) of a hypothetical investment:

Number of Periods (N): Enter 30 years as the time horizon.

Interest per Year (I/Y): Enter 10%, assuming a 10% annual return.

Present Value (PV): Enter $1,000,000 as your initial investment.

Periodic Payment (PMT): Enter 0, assuming no additional contributions.

Press Calculate.

The result is $17,449,402.27. This includes the initial investment, meaning the growth portion is $16,449,402.27—16.4 times the original amount.

---

[1]   https://www.calculator.net/finance-calculator.html

Now, compare this to a 4% annualized return:

Keep all the other numbers the same, but change the interest to 4%.

Press Calculate.

You get $3,243,397.51. The growth part is only $2,243,397.51, or about 2.2 times the original investment. Analyzing the two results, you find that the difference between 10% and 4% return over 30 years is a factor of 7, or 700%. That's the opportunity cost of earning less return over time—it directly impacts your future financial security.

Why Small Changes in Returns Matter

The above comparison shows how a seemingly small difference in annual return rates can make a monumental difference in long-term outcomes. Many investors underestimate how much even 1% or 2% difference in annual return rates can affect their nest egg over time. For example, a portfolio growing at 8% annually might feel like it's performing well, but if you have the opportunity to invest in assets that could generate 10% with a similar risk profile, you're leaving significant money on the table. Over 30 years, this could mean millions of dollars in lost wealth.

This is the essence of opportunity cost—it's not just about what you earn, but what you forgo. Every investment decision comes with a trade-off, and the impact of these trade-offs compounds over time.

The Power of Visualization and Motivation

Using a financial calculator isn't just a mathematical exercise; it's a motivational tool. When you see the potential growth of your investments laid out so clearly, it inspires action and careful planning. Let's take another example to see how different inputs affect your future wealth.

If you can set aside $100,000 each year for 30 years and achieve a 16% return, your portfolio will grow to an astounding $61.6 million. If that doesn't spark excitement, consider this: stretch the investment horizon to 40 years, and your portfolio will balloon to $274 million. Now, let's take it one step further—what if you could achieve an 18% annual return? After 40 years, your portfolio could reach $491 million.

These numbers are not just for dreaming; they represent what's possible with disciplined saving and intelligent investing. The quote "Begin with the end in mind," famously attributed to Stephen Covey, applies perfectly here. By visualizing your end goal, you can work backward to determine the inputs—like savings rate, investment returns, and time—that will get you there.

> *"Begin with the end in mind"*
>
> – Stephen Covey

Setting Audacious Goals

Now, let's get ambitious. What if your goal is to become a billionaire? Is that even remotely possible? The beauty of financial calculators is that they let you explore these "what-if" scenarios. Let's try one.

Say you've saved $120,000 and plan to contribute an additional $120,000 each year for the next 40 years. You aim for a future value of $1 billion. What return would you need to achieve this? Using the same online calculator:

N (Number of periods): 40 years.

PV (Present Value): -$120,000 (entered as a negative, since it's an outflow).

PMT (Periodic Payment): -$120,000 per year (also negative).

FV (Future Value): $1,000,000,000 (your goal).

Press Calculate.

The result is an annual return of 19.8%. While this might seem ambitious, it's not entirely out of reach. In fact, some investors have achieved annualized returns even higher than this through disciplined strategies and a bit of luck. In future chapters, we'll explore investment strategies that can help you aim for returns of 15%, 20%, or more, although such returns come with added risk and effort.

It's important to note that this doesn't mean you need to hit that annual return every year. This is an average return that is required. Some years may be worse than others, and some may even be negative.

This may be well beyond your means and even beyond your dreams. That's fine. If you're happy with the 7-8% annualized returns and want to stay safe and steady, there's nothing wrong with that. In fact, as we will soon discuss, each type of investment has unique risks. We have ways to mitigate the overall risk of the portfolio and of each holding, but some risks still remain.

The Trade-Offs of Opportunity Cost

Understanding opportunity cost goes beyond just comparing returns. It involves making strategic decisions about where to allocate your capital, what level of risk you're willing to take, and what sacrifices you're prepared to make for long-term rewards. For instance, investing in high-growth stocks or private equity may offer higher returns, but they come with greater volatility and risk. On the other hand, sticking with bonds or low-yield savings accounts may feel safer, but the opportunity cost of not exposing yourself to higher potential returns could drastically limit your wealth accumulation.

Opportunity cost also applies to how you manage your time and resources in pursuit of better returns. Do you have the time and energy to actively manage your investments, or would you be better off sticking with index funds or other passive strategies we'll discuss?

> *"The dream is free...but the journey will cost you something."*
>
> – John C. Maxwell

"There's no such thing as a free lunch."

– Milton Friedman

"Finding a single investment that will return 20% per year for 40 years tends to happen only in dreamland. In the real world, you uncover an opportunity, and then you compare other opportunities with that. And you only invest in the most attractive opportunities. That's your opportunity cost. That's what you learn in freshman economics. The game hasn't changed at all."

– Charlie Munger

Conclusion: Keeping Your Eye on the Prize

Opportunity cost is about more than just numbers—it's about mindset. Every choice you make today regarding your investments has a long-term impact. Whether you're targeting modest returns or aiming for audacious goals like becoming a billionaire, it's essential to understand the trade-offs involved in your decisions.

In the following chapters, we'll dive into the different investment methods that can help you achieve those returns and mitigate risks along the way.

CHAPTER #4

Prerequisites to Successful Investing

"Make sure you remember this: the people who now claim that the next "sure thing" will be health care, or energy, or real estate, or gold, are no more likely to be right in the end than the hypesters of high tech turned out to be."

– Benjamin Graham, The Intelligent Investor, 1949

After reviewing the initial three chapters, you may feel excited to jump into the stock market, believing that the indicators favor immediate investment. However, that's not my recommendation. Investing is highly personal, nuanced, and varies from person to person. It's essential to evaluate your individual circumstances, goals, and emotional preparedness before risking any money.

Assessing Your Unique Circumstances

The notion that everyone can adhere to the same investment advice is a myth. What proves effective for one individual might not be suitable for another, owing to variations in financial goals, risk appetite, and emotional temperament. This is why it can be perilous to follow media pundits or even well-intentioned online influencers without question. Unless someone has genuinely taken the time to comprehend your financial background, concerns, and ambitions, they are not equipped to provide you with trustworthy investment advice.

It's essential to recognize that your situation—financial and personal—is unlike anyone else's. For example, some investors may have a higher tolerance for risk, meaning they might be comfortable riding out market downturns. Others, particularly those approaching retirement or with dependents to support, may prefer a more conservative approach. Understanding your unique needs is the first step toward successful investing.

The Value of Mentors and Advisors

Investing, especially for long-term success, goes beyond selecting stocks or assets. A vital aspect is controlling your emotions. Fear, greed, and anxiety can obscure your judgment and result in poor decisions. This is why having an experienced mentor, coach, or financial advisor can be transformative. These professionals offer technical insights while also helping you manage the emotional ups and downs that come with investing.

A good advisor can help you create an investment strategy and adhere to it, even when the market becomes turbulent. Without an objective outside perspective, it's easy to make irrational decisions based on short-term market fluctuations or emotional responses. For instance, selling assets in a panic during a market downturn can cement losses that could have been avoided with patience. Likewise, an advisor can help you resist the temptation to chase trends when prices are climbing, potentially protecting you from buying in at inflated levels.

The Role of Robo-Advisors

Robo-advisors have become popular as a cost-effective solution for managing smaller investment portfolios. These automated platforms offer a straightforward, pre-set mix of assets, typically comprising index funds or ETFs, tailored to your risk tolerance. This approach works well for investors with less than $1 million, providing an accessible, low-maintenance investing method. However, robo-advisors do have limitations, particularly for high-net-worth individuals or those with more complex financial requirements.

For instance, robo-advisors overlook the emotional facets of investing. Although they may offer a basic allocation model, they cannot provide the human touch essential for managing the emotional ups and downs of fear and greed that frequently influence investor behavior. Furthermore, they lack the adaptability to recommend advanced strategies like covered calls or utilize alternative investments such as private REITs, private equity, or private loans, which can deliver important diversification and risk mitigation.

Why a Human Touch Still Matters

While technology has advanced significantly and AI is likely to play a larger role in the future, the human element remains irreplaceable for now. Conversations with a financial advisor can uncover ideas or strategies that might not be obvious through an algorithm. A professional can also help identify your blind spots, whether they relate to emotional tendencies or gaps in your financial knowledge. For example, an advisor might recommend using options strategies to hedge against potential losses or suggest diversifying into alternative investments to create a negative correlation with the stock market.

In addition to the benefits of having an accountability partner, allowing a reliable and experienced coach or advisor to help you make emotionally charged decisions can save you from headaches and heartache.

The Importance of Continuous Learning

Another key to successful investing is a continuous commitment to learning. Investing is not a one-size-fits-all endeavor; the strategies that work for one individual may not be suitable for another. The more you educate yourself, the better prepared you'll be to navigate the complexities of the market. This involves reading books and studying various investment strategies, from value investing to momentum investing.

Each approach has unique strengths. Value investing, for example, focuses on identifying companies that are undervalued by the market yet possess strong financials. Momentum investing, in contrast, involves capitalizing on trends by purchasing stocks that are already rising in price. Both strategies have their merits, but they attract different types of investors depending on their risk tolerance, investment horizon, and goals.

Understanding Different Investment Strategies

To expand on value vs. momentum investing, let's delve into what makes each unique. Value investors look at fundamentals, such as the price-to-earnings (P/E) ratio, or price-to-book value, to determine if a stock is undervalued. They are patient, waiting for the price to reflect the company's true worth. Momentum investors, by contrast, care more about the stock's price movement. They will jump on a stock that's rising quickly, hoping to ride the wave to further gains.

Book value is the value of a company's assets after netting out its liabilities.

The price-to-earnings (P/E) ratio measures a company's share price relative to its earnings per share (EPS). Often called the price or earnings multiple.

Here's an example using corn as a commodity. Suppose corn is currently trading at $4 per bushel. If the price drops to $3, a value investor would view this as a buying opportunity, as long as the fundamentals of the commodity still indicate strong long-term demand. However, a momentum investor would steer clear, since the downward trend suggests potential further losses. If the price jumps to $5 the following month, the momentum investor would get on board, while the value investor would only purchase if the underlying fundamentals also improved proportionally.

The key lies in understanding and discerning the various strategies and recognizing which one aligns with your personality and financial goals. This is just one example of the different strategies available there.

Once you understand these concepts, you'll be much more cautious before jumping into an investment simply because an online guru claims it's "going to the moon." First, you need to determine if the holding aligns with your investment goals, as well as your risk tolerance and time horizon.

Investing vs. Speculating

The road to success for investors has been littered with failures, some documented and many undocumented. As important as it is to learn from successful investors, it's equally important to see how failures develop so we can avoid them in our pursuit of success.

A frequent reason for the average investor's failure is that they were never truly investing; rather, they were speculating. They risked their hard-earned money on speculative ventures, leading to significant misfortune when those speculations turned unfavorable.

What's the difference?

In my practice, I take the time to help clients understand investing concepts. Every now and then, I'll hear a remark: "What do I care about the company? Whether it's a quality one or not, I just want one whose price is going up." or "All I care about is that it makes me money."

It's precisely this mentality that leads to speculation. If you aren't going to take the time to understand the company's fundamentals, how can you know if you're buying at a good price just because the stock price is climbing?

Benjamin Graham pioneered the distinction between investing and speculating in his groundbreaking work on value investing. Interestingly, during two different stages of his career, he contrasted investing and speculating from two opposing perspectives.

First, in the aftermath of the Great Depression in the 1930s, the stock market had turned into such a chaotic environment with widespread devastation that many believed all stocks were speculative. In their minds, only bonds could be considered safe enough to qualify as "investing." During that time, Graham argued that with thorough research and a solid understanding of the fundamentals and characteristics of a company, purchasing at the right price is not speculative and can indeed be regarded as "investing."

Years later, in his career, Graham had to defend against the contrary view when reckless investors were also being labeled as "investors." This occurred after the markets regained their footing and entered a state of euphoria. People were buying stocks solely based on their momentum, with prices rising disconnected from any fundamental valuation. It was then that Graham condemned those individuals as "speculators."

One lesson from Graham, that he so eloquently articulates in his parable of "Mr. Market," is that the market is a bipolar entity prone to significant mood swings throughout various seasons and years. Our job as investors is to act rationally and not be swayed by the market's fluctuations. Instead, we can take advantage of these extreme mood swings. While such behavior might be considered abusive in a real-life bipolar individual, it is completely moral when dealing with the stock market. When "Mr. Market" is in an extremely happy mood and demands high prices for everything, sell him your stocks. Conversely, when a year later, Mr. Market is depressed and willing to sell you everything for pennies on the dollar, buy as much from him as possible.

"Investors" make decisions grounded in the company's core fundamentals and are ready to purchase during downturns. In fact, this is the optimal time to buy. They aren't interested in buying the stock at its peak.

Those who "speculate" are usually jumping on the momentum wagon. When Mr. Market is at his happiest, they buy at market highs.

Among my recent transactions for clients was TSLA stock. We got in at $175 and sold out six months later at $480. I know many speculators were buying up the price in the $400 range based on momentum. However, to an investor looking at

> **"Investors" make decisions grounded in the company's core fundamentals and are ready to purchase during downturns. In fact, this is the optimal time to buy... "Speculators" jump on the momentum wagon, buying high flying instruments with little intrinsic value.**

the fundamentals, it made no sense to hold on at that point. Since getting out, now four months later, that stock has dropped 50% to the mid-low $200 range. To explain the rationale for entering at $175 would take us off-topic here. The point to take here is the need to be an independent thinker and be ready to sell when others are buying once you see the buying get irrational. When your investments are based on thorough investigative analysis, you are anchored in the safe haven of rational investing and won't get caught up in emotional folly.

Intrinsic Value

Warren Buffet differentiates between investments with intrinsic value and investments lacking intrinsic value.

Have you ever bought into an investment without regard for or thought of the yield or earnings created from the holding and how they relate to the demanded price? Was your only concern that someone else would pay you more for the item in the future?

This is typical for holdings that lack intrinsic value.

Intrinsic value is defined as something that would provide you with substantive value regardless of whether you'll be able to sell it to someone else. It doesn't always need to produce a yield via earnings, but that is definitely one way to assess the intrinsic value of an investment.

For instance, when you purchase a computer, you're not focused on how much you might sell it for to someone else. Your primary concern is the personal or business utility of the computer. The computer will deliver value through its use.

Similarly, if you bought a cow to produce milk, you would not be concerned about the ability to sell the cow at a higher price because the cow will create value for you every day for many years to come.

What about a meme coin? Can you say the same? Will there be a derived benefit if you never sell it to anyone else? Will meme coins have a collector's value down the road, similar to baseball cards?

When you look at the stock market with these glasses on, things become clear. We invest in companies that will produce a steady and growing stream of earnings that will pay out to shareholders for many years to come. We're not just buying a stock with the hope that it will go up in price in the near term to sell it at a higher price. You are evaluating the value of the business based on its ability to increase earnings over time. And you're looking at the current price compared to those earnings to ensure you're not overpaying for those expected earnings.

Accordingly, the same holding transaction can be an investment for one person and speculation for another. This is to say that the same stock holding, real estate holding, or any other type of investment for person A will be a great investment since he did his research and understands what's behind his purchase. However, for person B, this transaction will be speculative since his only interest was selling it to another investor at a higher price; he had no interest in understanding the underlying fundamentals.

Well, you may ask, what does it matter? If the same holding goes up in price, both person A and person B will make the same return. So, who cares if the transaction is labeled as "investing" or as "speculating"?

The difference is significant for the long-term investor. Since markets do not consistently rise over the long term, turbulence is inevitable. If you are a true "investor" focused on "intrinsic value," short-term price movements and market variability will not affect your level-headed decisions made after conducting thorough research and analysis. On the other hand, if you disregard intrinsic value and only purchase an asset to sell it to someone else at a higher price, you will be the first to divest and flee when market unpredictability arises.

This is not theoretical; this is the experience I have seen time and again. It is always fascinating that people who are extremely successful in life and in their careers and who are extremely smart in many other areas of intelligence will fail when it comes to these concepts. They will get into a holding with the sole interest of the price continuing its current climb, completely uninterested in the intrinsic value of the holding, and then be horror-stricken when markets take a nose dive.

The lesson is profound but simple: invest in holdings after you've conducted enough research that will allow you to hold through thick and thin. Markets are inherently volatile. If your investment decisions are anchored in a deep appreciation for the continued success of the company, the short-term fluctuations will not affect you and will only help you buy more at a lower price.

In contrast, meme coins are the complete opposite of something with intrinsic value. They are created based on a trend or someone's imaginative idea. They are fleeting, ephemeral, and lack any substance or actual purpose. You can't even hang one on your wall as a trophy; it's only digital. These are here today, gone tomorrow. Like the Non-Fungible Token (NFTs) fiasco, which was short-lived and is all but extinct.

It is amusing to see how many people get this wrong. How many people are throwing money into trends that will be short-lived.

Even if some very influential person is promoting the idea, it doesn't give it legitimacy.

If you are interested, you can find a list of the top meme coins trading on Forbes.com/digital-assets. This list shows how billions of dollars are traded daily on these short-lived holdings. Steer clear of this insane behavior!

Invest like Buying a New Car

When you purchase a new appliance or car, how much time will you take to research the purchase? Several weeks?

You'll likely visit the store or dealership, get a feel for the car, and then go online to read about the different features and compare it to other similar vehicles for several days. Once you have certainty about your choice, you'll call around to see if you're getting the best price. All of this will take a couple of weeks. You may even decide to wait for an upcoming date on the calendar when you're likely to find a better price.

Maybe I'm unique in this regard, but that's at least how I've been while making big purchases. The problem many people have is that they'll take weeks to research their new car or appliance, and then only a few minutes or hours to decide on a new investment. The reason is that, in their mind, the appliance is something they plan to live with for the next five, ten, or even 15 years, whereas the investment is just about holding it long enough to sell for a good return. So no serious time is required here, right? NO! Looking at the investment that way is pure speculation. Investing should take no less time and investigative work than the new appliance shopping expedition.

If you want to get a good sense of the company or holding, consider visiting a physical location and talking to some employees to understand the morale and mentality of the workforce. It's important to read about the management's history and their areas of expertise. What skills do they bring to the company? What are their visions for its future? Then, you might conclude that the company is worthy of investment, but you may get a better deal if you're patient—just like with purchasing a new car.

I always maintain a list of stocks that I've identified as strong companies, even though their current prices are too high. I keep this list for market pullbacks and take advantage of the volatility to jump on at good value for a company that, under normal circumstances, exceeds my buy price.

Discipline: The Backbone of Successful Investing

Discipline is the backbone of successful investing. It involves adhering to your investment plan, even when the market is volatile and the news is filled with doom and gloom. This demands not only the discipline to consistently contribute to your investment accounts but also to remain steadfast during market fluctuations and turbulence.

Markets can be unpredictable, and news that impacts stock prices can arise at any moment. Discipline helps you avoid panic selling during market downturns or overly exuberant buying during market peaks. By establishing clear rules for your investments—whether they involve asset allocation, stop-loss orders, or diversification—you can help reduce some of the risks inherent in the stock market.

Investing in risk assets is rarely with the "stars all lined up" perfectly. It's rare to get 100% clear skies. And there are usually grey areas of information. News can come out at any time that can change the trajectory of the stock market or of a particular stock/industry. There is no way to predict certain news. Even if the news were predictable, we don't always know how the market will react to the information. Sometimes, a company will beat earnings only for the stock to fall since the market didn't like one small part of what was reported.

A disciplined strategic approach is the answer to all this uncertainty. Discipline will help you establish rules to follow throughout the uncertainty.

> *"Nowadays people know the price of everything and the value of nothing"*
>
> – Oscar Wilde

Conclusion: The Journey to Successful Investing

Ultimately, successful investing is not just about finding the right stocks or funds to invest in. It's about preparing yourself mentally, emotionally, and financially for the journey. Invest in intrinsic value holdings that will pay you dividends for many years to come. Have a mentor or advisor who can guide you, continuously learn to stay informed, and maintain the discipline to follow your strategy through thick and thin.

CHAPTER #5

Stocks; Short and Long Term

"Blind obedience to authority is the greatest enemy of the truth."

– Albert Einstein

Where Many Go Wrong

Having covered the mindset and prerequisites necessary for effective investing, we can now delve into the different strategies and categories of holdings that are essential for building your retirement portfolio. For each category, we will highlight the common misconceptions and errors that many individuals encounter when utilizing that type of holding.

What goes into your portfolio?
Stocks
Bonds
ETFs
Mutual Funds
Private holdings, including;

Private Real Estate, rentals, rehab, construction.
Private Loans, including;
Mortgages, Bridging, high yield.
Private Equity
Stock Options; including covered calls and unique option spreads

Stocks

Regarding stocks, one of the most common issues is that investors often do not conduct their due diligence sufficiently and just buy the latest hot stock recommended by an online site or so-called "expert."

Sometimes, the recommended stock has already seen a nice rise and continues to trend upwards. Investors may join in a bit late, just when it seems to be turning around, missing the earlier opportunities.

Next thing they know, it declines by ten or twenty percent, causing the investor to panic and sell at a loss.

This happens more often than not. Professionals monitor the volume of stocks and can decipher when retail investors have joined. It is precisely then that the big pockets take the opposite position, as they know that the big move has already happened.

The issue with blindly following online recommendations is twofold:

One is that the investor didn't do independent research prior to investing but just relied on a third party. Even if multiple sources confirm that a particular investment is a good investment, if you don't do your own due diligence, which includes studying the income and balance sheets and comparing them to similar companies in their field, you are effectively relying on hearsay. The problem with hearsay is that you won't have the confidence or conviction to hold out when markets turn down.

Conversely, if you conduct your own research and, after investing time, you build confidence in the company, you'll be more likely to remain invested even when market fluctuations occur.

The second problem with buying based on some online site or guru is knowing when to sell. Is this a company you will hold forever, or is this a momentum play?

Even if the service tells you exactly what price to get in and what price to get out, you should be doing your own independent research to be successful and endure through thick and thin. These sites may be viewed by thousands of investors, and if the site or guru is really good, the idea may be watched by hundreds of thousands of investors around the world. That rush to a particular trade can itself move the markets and create additional artificial volume and volatility, which can lead to unexpected movements in various directions.

Instead, the safest way to buy is to examine the company's fundamentals: earnings per share, projected earnings growth over the next few years, and the health of the balance sheet and cash flow. Look for a good deal, not just a rising stock.

Knowing When to Buy

You also don't want to buy a stock on the way down, even if it appears to be a good deal. It's better to wait until it stops falling and then buy in once it starts to climb again. In other words, watch the trend; once the downtrend has reversed, it is ripe for buying, provided the fundamentals are all in place.

This is where technical and fundamental analysis intersect to identify the safest entry points. A stock may be declining and nearing a price range that could seem attractive for a purchase based solely on fundamentals. However, even if the price appears enticing, it's advisable to exercise patience and wait for a breakout above the downward trend. Otherwise, you risk trying to catch a "falling knife." While projected earnings might look strong, it's possible that the projected earnings could be reduced, and they may not appear as impressive in a few weeks as the stock continues to fall.

In a previous chapter, we discussed the difference between short term and long term investing and why it is crucial to be clear on which strategy you are pursuing. Clarifying the distinction between long-term and short-term strategies is essential because they are completely different.

Here is a breakdown of the differences:

Long Term	*Short Term*
Focus on the fundamentals	*Focus on the technicals, charts*
Look for the best value	*Look for direction*
Less concern about markets turning down for short periods	*Go with the market, get out if markets turn*
You must do an abundance of research on the quality of the company. Management should have an alignment with your values and be looking to create value over time.	*Importance of being agile, shift and pivot, don't ever go against the market.*

As you can see, the strategies are worlds apart. When investing in a long-term company, it's important to have conviction in the management's capabilities to grow the company nicely over time. When investing in a short-term company, you just need to confirm the direction—up or down— be agile and pivot, and not be smarter than the market.

Based on this, you can see how following the words of an online expert is unwise. He or she may be discussing a completely different strategy from what you are prepared to execute.

Defining the Time Frame

Long-term investments can be defined as lasting 5 to 10 years, with a minimum of five years. Generally, if you're investing your retirement nest egg, long-term investing is the better option. Short-term investing requires a lot of continuous monitoring and research, while long-term holdings offer the freedom to ignore the short-term noise of the market. This approach provides peace of mind and prevents the stress of feeling the need to worry about market fluctuations.

In long-term investing, you can spot outstanding companies with strong growth potential for the next decade and make sure you invest at a fair price. After that, you can relax and not look back very often. Just let the market do its thing. As long as projected earnings are growing and the company is in demand, it will grow over time. It's not so hard to find those companies that will surely grow over the coming ten or even twenty years. What is hard is to ensure you don't overpay for those companies.

What's a Reasonable Price?

It's clear that price isn't the only factor. A $10 stock isn't necessarily cheaper than a $90 stock simply due to its lower price. While it may seem humorous, I need to emphasize this point. I've heard people remark, "I don't invest in stocks over $100 because they're too pricey." That's utterly ridiculous! It's akin to saying, "I won't purchase shirts for more than $100, even if they come in a set of ten." If you typically buy shirts for $30 and can acquire ten of the same quality for $100, you've scored an excellent deal. When investing in stocks, we're effectively buying a bundle of future earnings. Let's see what's included in the bundle.

We start by examining price-to-earnings ratios. That is how many times earnings are included in the current price.

If stock A is selling for $100 and earning $5, that has a price-to-earnings ratio of 20. 100/5=20.

If stock B sells for $100 and earns $10, its price-to-earnings ratio is 10. 100/10 = 10.

Think of it like purchasing a business with a stream of future earnings. You always want to pay as little as possible for those future earnings. So, if stocks A and B are identical in every way, you should choose stock B, which has a lower price to earnings.

Next, we analyze earnings growth projections for the upcoming years. Analysts share this information with us and periodically update their guidance.

A company that consistently grows by 5% each year will be significantly more valuable than a company that maintains its current earnings over the next 5 to 10 years. Likewise, a company with a 15% annual growth rate will outshine one that grows at 5%.

Next, we will examine the company's balance sheet to assess its financial health. A critical aspect to consider is whether it carries significant debt, as this can impact its overall stability and future growth potential. Additionally, we will examine its cash flow situation, as it provides insight into its operational efficiency and ability to generate revenue.

This analysis is not merely a collection of numbers; rather, it forms a comprehensive overview of the company's financial landscape. By synthesizing this information, we can arrive at a more informed judgment about the reasonableness of the current market price.

Where Can Short-Term Trading Play a Role?

There is still room for short-term trading in your portfolio, but contrary to what you may have heard, it is generally much riskier. This is because it requires perfectly timing the market and understanding its direction, which is an imprecise art and science. There's also a lot more babysitting and monitoring to do.

To make the time worth the effort, many short-term traders use leverage techniques that effectively exponentially increase the risk-reward profile of short-term holdings. We will discuss one such strategy, call options and put options, later on. Another example of leverage that short-term investors use is futures. With futures, an investor can purchase one contract for several hundred dollars; a contract of the SP500 will represent 50 times the actual value of one SP500, meaning about $300,000 in assets. If the investor wants to hold the contract overnight, they will need to provide more margin or deposited funds, which typically range from $15,000 to $25,000, depending on the brokerage. Thus, with 15K, you can control 300K in assets. This results in a leverage ratio of 1 to 20. That is, each $1 invested controls $20.

Due to leverage, a 10% change in SP500 can yield a gain of 30K, resulting in a 200% return on your 15K deposit. Conversely, for every 1% drop, you will lose 3K from your account, requiring you to deposit this amount to meet the margin requirement. A 5% decline could wipe out your entire 15K. This illustrates the exponential impact of leverage.

In real estate, we often utilize leverage through mortgages. When you make a 20% down payment on a home and finance the remaining 80% with a mortgage, you're effectively employing a 1 to 5 leverage ratio. Conversely, if you secure a 95% loan, this represents a 1 to 20 leverage ratio.

This leverage in the futures market primarily caters to short-term investors. Because tracking fluctuations and deciding optimal entry and exit points requires considerable effort, these investors often capitalize on leverage to amplify their potential returns, as price movements tend to be minor.

The short-term investor needs to be extremely in tune with the market's rhythm. The market can be likened to a dancer performing a self-created dance. At times, the dance will appear magnificently orchestrated, with each move predictable. At other times, the dancer may seem almost drunk, moving in random, disorganized directions.

It is the objective of the short-term trader to jump into the dance when it seems organized and predictable and to stay on the sidelines when randomness and chaotic fluctuations abound.

Here is another perspective on the short-term trader's necessary skillset for analyzing price movements and the accompanying technical indicators, such as volume, on the charts. The market often communicates in multiple languages simultaneously. I don't mean English and Chinese; I'm referring to the social cues that emerge during a conversation. When people talk, many factors come into play for those familiar with body language. There are tonalities, postures, and a range of facial expressions to observe in addition to the spoken words. At times, body language, postures, and facial expressions can convey a message that holds greater significance than the verbal information. This message may, at first glance, even contradict the verbal one, but once aligned, it can clarify that both were true, just in different ways. One refers to the immediate future, while the other points to the distant future.

Similarly, the equity market emits many different cues simultaneously. Often, the cues are conflicting and not in sync with one another. The skill of the short-term trader is to sift through the cues, distinguish the important ones from the unimportant ones, and try to understand what the market is indicating about its next move or dance direction.

For the long-term investor, all the dance, posters, body language, etc., is just noise. There is no reason to pay attention to it. The long-term investor has no use for studying the short-term noise of the markets.

In general, investing in stocks requires the ability to handle large swings. For short-term investors using the leverage mentioned, these swings can decimate the investor. But for long-term investors without leverage, the swings will eventually return to usual composure, and all will be well.

How to Deal with Volatility

Let's return to the long-term investor. It's important to ask whether you can endure significant market fluctuations with each equity position. Relying on exiting the stock market after news suggests it's time to sell is a risky approach; by that point, it is typically too late, and holding onto your investment may be wiser. Thus, a long-term investor must exhibit patience and ride out market volatility during downturns. By anticipating potential swings in a position, investors can determine their tolerance levels and the appropriate investment amount for that holding. This understanding is fundamental to effective portfolio construction aimed at long-term success, as it informs in advance how much to allocate to each asset class. Each asset will likely increase in value over time; it's the short-term panic we need to protect ourselves from.

Here's an example to illustrate the need for long-term investors to hold through the market cycle:

We've experienced several big swings over the last few years, but let's analyze the last major one.

At the end of 2021, the market had reached a new all-time high. Over the following 10 months, as inflation rose to 8-9% and interest rates soared, the market entered a downward cycle. By October 2022, the market had declined about 26% from its peak. This means your $1 million was now worth $740,000, your $10 million was worth $7.4 million, and your $30 million was worth approximately $22 million. You get the point. This is a lot of money!

When do you think you might have chosen to sell? I can confidently say that it's unlikely you would have sold at the peak at the end of 2021 or the start of 2022. How would you go about deciding to sell if the market continues to climb?

You would also resist any call to sell on the first leg down (March 2022-see chart) because that is no proof that we are in a sustained down market. It was only once we had the second leg down, with each high lower than the prior high and each low lower than the prior low, that you would feel the urge, based on the news and media pundits, to get out. This was around April 2022, six months before the bottom. By then, you were 14% off the high.

So, let's imagine you sold off in April 2022. The next question is: when will you be ready to jump back in? Again, I can tell you with certainty that you won't buy back in at the bottom in October 2022. How do I know? If the market is hitting new lows, how can you jump in?

Once again, you would not re-enter during the first leg up because there is no solid evidence that we are out of the woods. Only after the second leg up do we see each low higher than the previous low and each high higher than the last high. Now, the media pundits are saying it's time to get back in, but by then, we're already 20% off the low. This was in May of 2023. In addition to the high likelihood that you would be buying back in at a higher price than what you sold for, you would also likely be worse off due to the realized gains tax, unless your account was held entirely in an RRSP or another tax-exempt account.

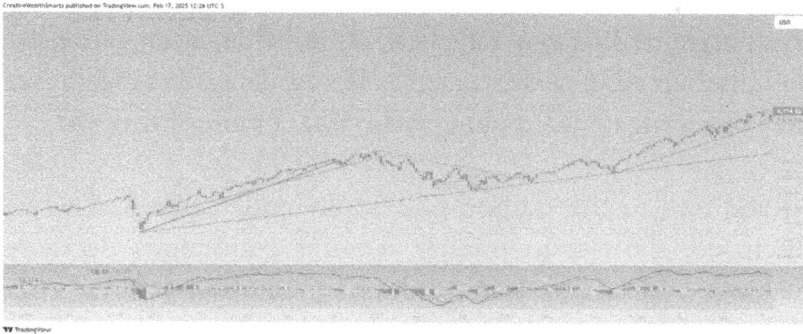

The lesson is that long-term investors should avoid attempting to time their market entries and exits. Instead, since you plan to invest for the long term, concentrate on quality holdings that can withstand market fluctuations. This requires thorough research and due diligence. You've evaluated the earnings, balance sheet, and other key fundamentals, and the company's management seems effective, with long-term goals that enhance shareholder growth.

There's nothing wrong with being a short-term trader who aims to capture the market's directional movement if that's your preference and cup of tea. However, it will require more time and attention, as well as active monitoring of the market or stock you intend to trade. You will need to exert a lot more energy, and it may or may not pay off in the end.

One must remember that markets often send mixed and conflicting signals, particularly amid the short-term noise. Data shows that many short-term traders encounter considerable difficulties, with approximately 80% losing 80% of their capital within a mere 80 days. Although this statistic may actually be overstated, it underscores a crucial truth: achieving success in short-term trading generally benefits individuals who are adept and disciplined in their strategies. Recognizing this insight can help one navigate the trading environment more effectively!

In addition to the trading philosophy and required skills we discussed, short-term trading requires continuous decision-making, which can lead to human emotions taking over. Therefore, it is critical to remain rational and not allow folly to overtake us while short-term trading.

Ultimately, adopting a long-term investment strategy is likely to provide more reassurance for most of your equity exposure as you learn to overlook the market's fluctuations. Over time, you can expect a growing asset with compounded returns as long as you avoid high-priced entries, patiently wait for the right entry point, and conduct thorough research before making any purchases.

In Conclusion

Whether you're a long-term investor or a short-term trader, what portion of your retirement savings are you comfortable investing in equities? It's natural for market fluctuations to happen, and there may be some years when we see significant declines. What level of risk feels right for you? The great news is, you don't have to choose an all-or-nothing approach! As we'll discover together, a key strategy is to diversify across different types of assets, each responding uniquely to economic changes. While we expect each chosen asset class to perform well and provide good returns over time, they each come with their own unique short-term risks. This diversification strategy can help create a more balanced investment journey, making it easier for you to stay focused on your long-term goals. Together, we'll delve into how successful diversification relies on ensuring negative correlations—essentially, making sure the risks of each asset class don't move in sync with others in your portfolio. This negative correlation helps smooth out the overall risks and volatility, allowing you, the investor, to navigate through tougher times with greater ease.

While we expect each chosen asset class to perform well and provide good returns over time, they each come with their own unique short-term risks.

CHAPTER #6

Stock Due Diligence

"My attitude is that I always want to be better prepared than someone I'm competing against. The way I prepare myself is by doing my work each night."

— Marty Schwartz

We have been discussing the necessity of conducting proper due diligence when making an investment. We will now cover three distinct types of analytical research that you will need to perform:

1. Fundamental
2. Technical
3. Analysts reviews

Fundamental Analysis

Let's start with fundamental analysis. There are numerous books on this topic, and covering everything in one chapter is quite challenging. Nevertheless, the essentials of the matter are outlined below.

We start with looking up the past and projected future earnings of a company. There are many online sites where you can get such information.

When looking up earnings, you'll often find that the figures shown online are not the same as those on the company's income statement. The reason for the discrepancy is that online sites adjust the earnings to weed out one-time transactions or non-recurring earnings and losses so that you can quickly see the trend of the core business over time.

It's important to see the adjusted earnings growing over time. But if they had a bad year in the past, even the most recent one, that's okay. The future is much more important because what happened in the past has already been reflected in the current price. You may even be getting a discounted stock because of some recent mishap.

We're looking for growing earnings, which is very important. If a company's earnings remain stagnant, its stock will eventually fall.

Next, we want the growth to be at least high single digits, if not double digits, meaning close to 10% or greater on an annual basis. The way to determine this is by using a calculator: type in next year's projected earnings, then divide it by this year's earnings. For example, if next year's earnings are $10 per share and this year's were $9 per share, you get 10/9 = 1.11; this tells us that earnings are projected to grow by 11%. It's important to do this for the coming few years. You want to see the projected earnings growing. However, a note of caution: the projected earnings will be based on a number of analysts who are doing their deep dives and coming up with a best estimate for the future. The problem is that not all analysts are willing to project several years into the future. So, many times, the online portal will show year 3 or 4 with lower or plateaued earnings, while in essence, it's just the lack of analysts working that far out.

The next step is to compare the projected earnings to the current price by dividing the price by the earnings. For example, if the stock is priced at $100 and the earnings are $9, we calculate 100/9 = 11.1. This indicates that the stock is trading at 11.1 times its earnings. This is known as the P/E ratio, or price-to-earnings ratio.

A lower P/E ratio suggests better valuation, assuming all else is equal. However, a very low P/E ratio could signal potential concerns to consider.

Conversely, a current P/E ratio of 25 might appear elevated. It's wise to project the P/E ratio based on future earnings. You might think that this year's P/E is high, but you might choose to invest at this level if the anticipated growth in the upcoming years justifies it.

Like earnings, revenue growth is similarly essential. If earnings are growing but revenue appears flat, or if earnings are increasing by 12% each year while revenue only grows by 2%, it raises questions about the quality of those earnings.

Next, check the balance sheet. Is the debt manageable or high? Is it growing or shrinking? Growing debt is not a good sign in most cases unless the company has been borrowing to increase earnings and believes the new earnings potential far outweighs the interest costs.

The structure of debt and equity in a company is crucial to understanding the inherent risks. Similar to owning a house, there are two components to the financial ownership framework. First, there is the mortgage owed to the bank, and second, there is the equity you have in the home. The mortgage enables you to buy a larger home than what you could afford with cash alone. This represents your leverage. By securing a 60% mortgage, you effectively own only 40% of the home, while the bank holds the remaining balance. As long as you consistently make your mortgage payments, the bank will be satisfied, and everything will proceed smoothly. Eventually, as you pay down your mortgage, you will become the full owner of 100% of the home.

Businesses will similarly borrow to invest and grow, and as long as their cash flow is adequate to cover all the payments related to the loans, they will be fine. However, it is critically prudent to analyze the structure and percentage of equity to debt. Even if the current cash flow is more than sufficient to cover all debt obligations, a large amount of debt can weigh on the future viability of the company if it experiences a rough time or if the economy is unstable. Therefore, debt is a double-edged sword; on the one hand, it can accelerate growth by allowing the company to invest in new opportunities without current cash on hand. On the other hand, when the economy faces challenges, this same debt can drag them down.

Technical Analysis

What is technical analysis? Unlike fundamental analysis, which focuses on the inner workings of a company, starting with its earnings and revenue along with its other accounting statements to help create a value-based assessment of what the company should be worth or trading at, technical analysis looks at historical price movement. When projected on a chart, we can see if the price is going up or down, as well as when the price experienced support on the bottom downside or resistance on the top upside. We can also observe the volume of market participants, noting when more participants stepped in to support the move and when there was less interest in trading the holding.

Technical tools can be layered onto a chart to help interpret market direction, and each requires its own dedicated study. However, the primary objective of all technical analysis is to determine the direction of the next move.

Both fundamental and technical analysis are important and helpful in determining whether to purchase a stock investment. Generally, fundamentals provide a good idea of a stock's value and whether it is inexpensive or expensive based on its earnings and projected earnings growth. Technicals, on the other hand, examine the stock's trend or direction on the chart. After concluding that the fundamentals are sound, you should check if the stock has recently pulled back and may be poised for an upward reversal.

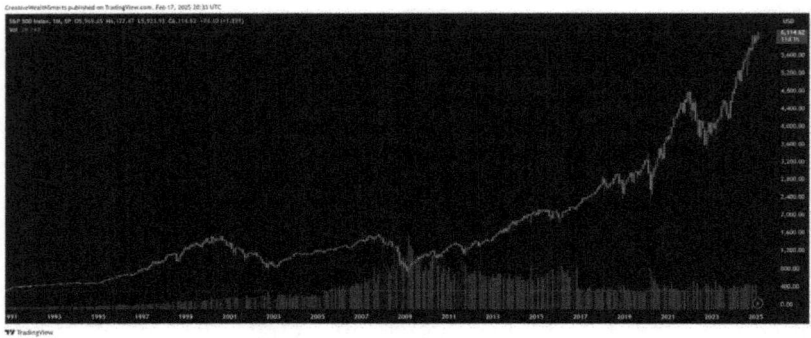

Here is a monthly bar chart of the S&P 500 dating back to 1991. Although the long-term trend is up, there have been many pullbacks over the years.

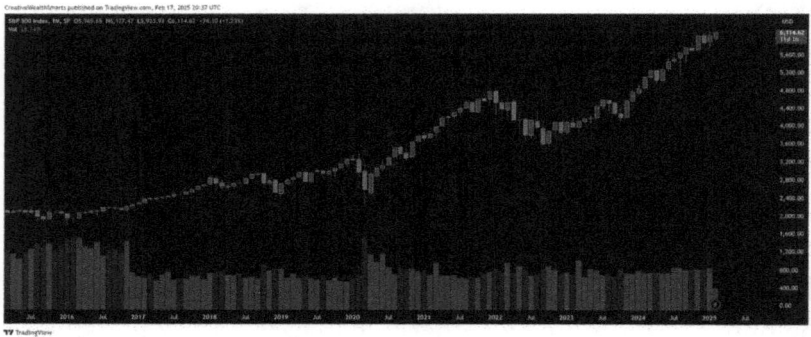

When we zoom in, we observe the pullback during the early COVID period in February and March 2020. While it appears minor here, it caused significant panic in the markets, resulting in a decline of over 30% in a very brief period.

Reading a chart is an essential skill in stock analysis, blending both art and science to inform investment decisions. By analyzing price movements and patterns over time, investors can gain insights into market behaviors and potential future trends. This process involves various elements, including identifying support and resistance levels, moving averages, and trendlines, which can indicate whether a stock is likely to rise or fall.

One key component of chart reading is understanding volume, which shows the number of shares traded during a specific period. High trading volume can suggest a strong interest in a stock and validate the trend, while low volume might indicate weakness in the price movement. Additionally, chart patterns such as head-and-shoulders, flags, and double tops can signal potential reversals or continuations in the stock's price trajectory.

Moreover, integrating technical indicators, such as the Relative Strength Index (RSI) or moving average convergence divergence (MACD), can enhance the analysis and further confirm market trends.

While reading charts does not guarantee profits, it equips investors with the tools to make informed predictions about market behavior, helping them navigate the complexities of investing with greater confidence.

Analysts' Reviews

In addition to the previously mentioned types of analysis, we should also consider insights from other analysts. These experts have conducted extensive research on the stock you are interested in, and understanding their perspectives can be beneficial. However, with the vast number of websites available, anyone can post recent news and assert their knowledge about a stock's details, often adding personal biases or agendas. To an inexperienced investor, the second-hand reporter and the credible analyst may seem indistinguishable. How can you differentiate between them?

How can we distinguish quality research or reporting from biased secondhand news commentary?

First, check the individual's qualifications. Have they studied to be an analyst or just to be a journalist? Or, worse yet, do they have neither?

Next, are they working for a reputable analytical company? Have they been assigned to analyze a specific type of holding? This is the best indicator. If not, just dismiss them.

It should also indicate somewhere in the analysts' work that they are prohibited from taking a position in the securities they are reporting on. Alternatively, if they are a fund company, they should fully disclose their position disclosure.

Unfortunately, there exists a group of commentators whose primary aim is to exploit the public by artificially inflating a stock's price after they have already invested. They make unrealistic claims about these stocks, only to sell or short their positions once the prices peak, allowing them to profit both during the rise and the subsequent decline. Tragically, speculative investors often chase this hype and end up falling into a trap.

When discussing traps, there are two others that are not related to bad actors; they are simply factors of the market that we need to be familiar with. These are the value trap and the momentum trap. These are really two complete opposites.

A value trap is a type of stock that may initially appear attractive to investors due to a low price-to-earnings ratio and the potential for a strong dividend yield. However, these positive indicators can be misleading. Often, a value trap exists because the company's fundamentals are in decline—the business may be struggling, and its management may lack effectiveness. This situation can fool investors into thinking they are securing a great deal when, in fact, the stock's value is likely to depreciate over time. Consequently, some investors might erroneously buy into the stock expecting it to rebound, only to see it continue to decline. In some cases, they may even purchase additional shares under the impression that the stock is an even better bargain as it drops further in value.

On the other hand, a momentum trap involves stocks that are experiencing rapid price increases, capturing the attention of investors. Despite the rising prices, the underlying earnings of the company may not be matching this growth, or the earnings growth may be insufficient to justify the soaring stock price. The disconnect between price and earnings can lead investors to believe that something significant is happening within the company that they may not yet understand. This belief encourages many average investors to jump on the momentum bandwagon, often right before the stock experiences a downturn as reality catches up with the unsustainable price growth.

In Summary:

Stock analysis requires examining a company from various perspectives. You must comprehend the company's income and balance sheets, as well as its cash flow and projected earnings. Additionally, evaluate the management's skills and their level of creative competence. You should also analyze the charts to grasp the projected price direction. Furthermore, avoid pitfalls that can derail even the most promising opportunities. Much of this work is an ongoing adventure. Even after buying into the investment, once you've conducted your analysis on a stock, it's crucial to ensure that the underlying story remains consistent.

CHAPTER 7

Shield Your Portfolio from Volatility Using Alternatives to Equities

---

"An ounce of prevention is worth a pound of cure."

– Benjamin Franklin

"Great spirits have always encountered violent opposition from mediocre minds."

– Albert Einstein

Why Alternatives?

What is your objective with your portfolio? Do you want the highest possible return or the highest possible return for the optimal amount of risk?

The difference between the two is like night and day! If your main focus is on achieving the highest return, it's important to keep in mind that this might come with a fair amount of risk to make it happen.

I consistently aim to set my clients on a path toward lasting success. Achieving long-term success involves generating reliable, quality returns year after year over several years. When clients express a desire for a rapid, high return of, say, 20%, I illustrate how they can quadruple their investments in 15 years with an annual compounded rate of 9.7%. You don't need to take on so much risk to achieve a great outcome. This typically encourages them to remain committed to the program. If you prefer to aim for a 15% annual return, we can pursue that as well, but it will come with a higher level of risk.

If our objective is to maximize returns for a given level of risk, we start with a conscious understanding of that risk and develop our strategies while being mindful of our risk tolerance.

If our main objective is achieving the highest possible return on investment, then incorporating stocks as the main component of your portfolio is likely the most advantageous strategy. Stocks have historically outperformed other asset classes over the long term, offering substantial growth opportunities. If you really want the highest potential return, you might consider utilizing options trading as a method to further amplify returns through leveraged positions and strategic plays. However, it's essential to note that this approach is not universally advisable, as it carries increased risk and complexity that may not be suitable for every investor.

To create a more balanced investment approach, especially for those who are risk-conscious, it's prudent to diversify your portfolio by including other asset classes, such as bonds, real estate, or commodities. This diversification acts as a buffer, helping to mitigate potential losses when the economy experiences downturns or volatility. By blending stocks with these alternative holdings, you can achieve a more stable investment strategy while still positioning yourself for growth.

Bonds

Many investors believe bonds cannot provide a good return. At best, people assume they will yield one to two percentage points above the rate of GICs. While it's true that bonds from large-cap companies typically pay a low yield, numerous bond opportunities can actually serve as excellent holdings, as long as you are prepared to conduct your due diligence. It is quite common to discover 8-10% bonds from companies with solid balance sheets and strong earnings. This essentially means you will achieve close to the long-term average return of the SP500 without all the volatility.

In addition to diversifying your risk, this can also enhance your peace of mind. Bonds tend to perform more favorably during economic downturns than the stock market. The reason is that bonds have a prior claim on a company's revenues before any shareholders can receive or realize their value. So, when the stock is rising, the bond does not participate in the growth that benefits the shareholders. However, if the company faces difficulties, the shareholders will be the first to be impacted, while creditors will generally be protected as long as there is enough revenue to meet the debt obligations.

There is a second reason why bonds tend to perform well during economic downturns. When the economy struggles, central banks often lower interest rates to stimulate growth. Bonds typically pay a fixed income, providing investors with a steady stream of revenue over time. As interest rates decrease, the fixed payments from existing bonds become relatively more attractive to investors compared to newly issued bonds that would pay lower rates. This increased demand for existing bonds causes their prices to rise. Investors looking for stability during uncertain economic times may increasingly turn to bonds, knowing that these investments can provide a reliable income even when other sectors of the market are faltering. Therefore, the steady income and relative safety of bonds during downturns reinforce their value and drive up their prices in a falling interest rate environment.

How to Pick Companies for your Bond Allocations?

I rarely invest in the same company's stock and bond at the same time. The reason is that, for the most part, my stock allocations are in companies that not only have a steady balance sheet but also have growing projected revenues and earnings. This is important for successful stock allocations. You need the earnings to grow over time, which will in turn increase the stock price. Even if they grow at the rate of inflation, that will not suffice. We need the companies to grow earnings beyond the rate of inflation year after year for the stock to grow.

However, for bonds, you don't necessarily need the earnings to grow over time, at least not significantly. As long as their balance sheet is stable and their income covers their debt obligations, they will be fine in terms of their bonds. It's this distinction that will allow you to get a good return on the bonds. If you only invest in the bonds of blue-chip growing companies, you will only receive a small yield, about 1-2% above the rate of GICs.

Mutual Funds and Exchange Traded Funds

Mutual funds can be a good way to gain bond exposure. Since there is little online analysis of the bond market available for retail investors, it's often better to obtain bond exposure through a mutual fund.

At times, you may want exposure to a specific geographic location (e.g., India) but lack the ability to invest directly. Alternatively, you might want to invest in a particular industry (e.g., semiconductors) as a whole without dealing with individual stock holdings. ETFs are great for this, allowing investors to enjoy unique exposure with built-in diversification across tens or hundreds of holdings.

There may also be times when you desire a managed solution based on certain momentum or value criteria but don't have enough resources to oversee individual stocks. Mutual funds can assist you in this regard. Like exchange-traded funds, they provide built-in diversification across hundreds of holdings and are managed according to the unique mandate and skills of the fund manager.

However, a word of caution regarding ETFs and mutual funds: many people seek a mutual fund that has significantly risen recently. This can lead to disastrous outcomes, as the stock holdings may have already peaked. Even if the fund is actively managed with constant buying and selling, the style or industry may have exhausted its growth potential for the foreseeable future. It might even be due for a pullback in the near term.

With individual stocks, you can assess this based on the P/E ratio and the historic P/E of the stock, as well as technical charts. These indicators will show you if a stock is at a peak and in need of a breather. Ideally, you want to invest in quality stocks after they've had a downturn due to specific news that has run its course, positioning the stock for a potential rebound upward. However, in the context of mutual funds, that kind of analysis is virtually impossible since you're dealing with hundreds of holdings at once. The method typically employed for investing in mutual funds with a recent track record of strong returns can be problematic.

Alternative Investments

Generally, alternative investments refer to holdings that don't trade on a public exchange and aren't easily accessible through a central exchange platform. These include private loans, private REITs, private equity, and similar holdings.

Private Loans

Unlike bonds, which are typically for medium to large-sized companies, the private lending market focuses on smaller entities. These include mortgages for individuals and companies, as well as short-term loans for businesses and similar lending structures. There are many different managers in this space; some are competent, while others are far from adequate. This market presents a wide spectrum, with some situations so concerning that regulators must intervene and take control of the assets. Management must excel not only in the lending aspect of the business but also in managing the assets if the loan outcomes deteriorate.

Additionally, it is important to understand what security is being offered for the loan. If it is secured against property, what is the loan-to-value ratio? There are also distinctions between securing built property versus land. Land can lose value quickly during an economic downturn, whereas a well-maintained built property is likely to "weather the storm."

In addition to the risks associated with loans, the limited regulatory oversight in the alternative space makes it crucial to ensure the integrity of management and the staff you are interacting with.

Private REITS

These include corporations that manage portfolios of real estate holdings that do not trade on a stock exchange. These portfolios can consist of rental units across multiple geographic jurisdictions. The managers of these portfolios possess expertise in identifying undervalued properties and enhancing their value over time, fixing inefficiencies, and increasing rental income. This ultimately leads to favorable returns for the investors.

Some of these Real Estate Investment Trusts will invest in new construction ventures. While these new buildings may provide greater returns than rental unit ventures, they come with a higher degree of risk, as new construction is less predictable. More things can go wrong, or costs may exceed initial expectations.

It is crucial to know the builders' past history and the fund's management tenure regarding their previous projects in this space.

One of the most appealing advantages of Private Loans and Private REITs is that they usually maintain a steady unit price, also referred to as the NAV. This is the price at which you buy or sell the units. Unlike public exchanges, which are constantly fluctuating, these private holdings remain quite stable. This means that when the market experiences a bad month or year, and the stock market drops by 20%, these will continue to grow steadily. Even the bond market is consistently in flux and adjusts to new economic developments. In contrast, these loans do not adjust in the same manner.

The lack of movement in these private holdings is due to the fact that they do not trade on a public exchange. When an asset is exposed to the price fluctuations of a public exchange, it will continually adjust to investor sentiment. New information is always circulating, causing prices to fluctuate. If fear dominates market sentiment, it can lead to a downward spiral of price movement.

On the other hand, these holdings are not tradable on an exchange, and the price of units is based on accountants and auditors evaluating the value of the loans or real estate holdings. This is the sole determining factor for pricing. It is precisely this absence of whimsical price movements that makes them appealing. However, to maintain this price stability, management may need to gate the fund at times, meaning they disallow a mass exodus of investors simultaneously. Many such funds stipulate that they will not allow more than 3-5% of the total invested assets to be redeemed at any one time.

Some people might ask, if private REITs and Loans provide the same average return as the stock market, why not invest everything in these two types of holdings without any other exposure? Why would one want any exposure to the stock market at all?

It is important to remember that every investment carries some risk. The only risk-free return comes from government-guaranteed assets, such as GICs. Anything providing a return above the rate of a GIC carries risk. These investments do have risks. Our job is to mitigate those risks as much as possible, which will be discussed in greater detail.

One of the significant risks in this space is the lack of regulatory oversight, which can potentially lead to bad actors. This is also why such investments are generally reserved for investors with high incomes or substantial asset bases. Furthermore, any retail investor buying into one of these funds must sign a document with extensive fine print regarding the inherent risks involved. One line is usually bold: YOU CAN LOSE ALL YOUR MONEY. When investing in typical stocks or bonds, no such acknowledgment is required.

Nonetheless, if you conduct proper research, these investments can prove to be great long-term holdings.

Private Equity

Various strategies and methods can be used to invest in private equity, each catering to different types of investors and goals. A crucial factor for success in private equity investments is the quality of management—specifically, the talent, skill, and integrity of the management team running the fund. Their ability to make informed decisions and manage the investment portfolio directly affects the fund's performance.

Additionally, the risks associated with private equity investments resemble those of other alternative investments. These risks may include market volatility, illiquidity, and the potential for fluctuations in the valuation of the underlying assets. Understanding these risks is essential for investors as they navigate the complexities of the private equity landscape, ultimately influencing their investment strategy and outcomes.

In conclusion, incorporating alternative holdings into an investment portfolio serves a crucial function in navigating the unpredictable landscape of equity markets. One of the primary advantages of this approach is its ability to mitigate volatility. By integrating various asset classes or baskets of holdings—such as real estate, commodities, or fixed-income securities—investors can create a more balanced and resilient portfolio. These alternative assets can maintain their value or even appreciate during market downturns, effectively providing a safeguard when equities experience significant declines, such as a 20% drop in any given year.

Furthermore, alternative holdings not only help in reducing risk but also enhance the potential for returns in the long term. Diversification across different asset categories can lead to improved overall performance, as these assets often react differently to economic shifts. This strategy enables investors to smooth out their returns, ensuring that their financial goals remain attainable even in challenging market conditions. Overall, the incorporation of alternative holdings is a prudent strategy for investors seeking stability and growth in an ever-changing financial environment.

CHAPTER #8

Stock Options

"There is no single market secret to discover, no single correct way to trade the markets. Those seeking the one true answer to the markets haven't even gotten as far as asking the right question, let alone getting the right answer."
— Jack Schwager – Author of Market Wizards

Options serve as a significant financial instrument, providing unique opportunities for investors to enhance their portfolios. However, this potential comes with a requirement for caution, as many people mishandle options, leading to considerable financial setbacks. For novice investors, the thrill of entering options trading can feel as intense as that caused by powerful drugs like fentanyl, especially when compared to less intense alternatives.

This allure stems from the potential for enormous gains that options offer, making them far more enticing than traditional stock market investments. The thrill of options trading lies in the possibility of amplifying your bets on market movements, often within short timeframes. The speed with which options trading operates, with rapid price fluctuations and the ability to capitalize on events quickly, can be dramatically faster than the relatively stable environment of the traditional stock market.

Furthermore, the intricate nature of options strategies may foster a misleading sense of safety, causing numerous investors to overlook the associated risks. This oversight can result in impulsive choices based on emotions instead of informed analysis. For individuals who are not well-versed in options' complexities, it is vital to proceed carefully and thoroughly educate themselves about the underlying mechanics and possible outcomes. This careful approach is essential for successful options trading.

Nevertheless, certain strategies can greatly enhance returns and lower risk exposure when implemented effectively. I particularly enjoy using the covered call and Debit Call Spread strategies. However, each of those needs to be executed with finesse to be successful.

Option Strategies

There are many different option strategies that can all yield a good return. The key is to know when to use which strategy and how to execute it efficiently.

Here, we'll cover four strategies I have used successfully over the years:

Long Call
Covered Call

Long Put
Debit Call Spread

Although the first three can be considered basic or entry-level, effectively executing them to achieve a good return is anything but a basic skill. In fact, many other "advanced" options strategies demand less expertise, as they do not require the ability to accurately predict and capture the right direction of the stock.

Long Call and Long Put strategies require the ability to predict the direction of the market within a certain timeframe.

Unlike buying the stock outright, the call option has an expiry date. When you buy the call, you pay a premium based on the time until expiration. The shorter the time, the lower the premium. The longer the time, the higher the premium.

Similarly, regarding the long put position, the put option is intended to be bought only when you believe the stock will decline in the near term. Conversely, the call option is intended to be purchased only when you anticipate the stock will rise in the near future.

Why would you want to buy a call option with a time premium that decays over the remaining time until expiration? Shouldn't you just buy the underlying stock outright? This way, you don't need to predict anything in the short term.

In a single word, the answer is leverage.

Say stock ABC is trading at $100. If you were to buy 100 shares, it would cost you $10,000. If the stock goes up to $110 in the coming month, you would have achieved a remarkable 10% return, giving you an extra $1,000. That's amazing! Right? But if you felt strongly that the stock was going to make that kind of move in the short term, you could have bought a call option on this stock. You can choose an expiration of one week, one month, or one year, whatever makes sense based on how you see the stock playing out. Say you decide to buy the $100 strike price, which is considered "at the money" (the price of the stock at the time of purchase). The one-month expiration has a premium of $5. One call unit includes 100 stock options, so the cost is 100 x $5 = $500. Over the next 30 days, the stock rises to $110. Now your call option is worth $10 because it gives you the right to buy the stock at $100 price.

Your $500 investment has now doubled in value to $1,000! That's a 100% return!

This is the meaning of leverage.

You can either turn your $10,000 into $11,000 for a 10% return. Or into $20,000 for a 100% return.

A note of caution:

Earlier, we discussed the difference between investing and speculating. We highlighted the damage that can occur from confusing the two. If you buy a long-term investment without conducting research, simply assuming that the price will rise, that is speculating, and the associated dangers were explained earlier.

Understanding this distinction is crucial for making informed decisions in the market.

Buying a call option is a form of speculation. This cannot be considered an "investment" in the true sense of the word, as explained by Ben Graham's definition. In general, short-term trading, the way it's usually done, isn't really investing. Any short-term position is effectively speculation. You are speculating that the stock will move in your favor during the short term. Unlike long-term investing, where you recognize the intrinsic value of the holding through its potential earnings and the growth of those earnings over time, with short-term holdings, you don't really care about intrinsic value. Your only concern is that the price goes up until the short-term duration ends.

As long as you understand the differences, there is no "sin" in trading a short-term holding. You just need to be keenly aware of the price and the underlying fundamentals to ensure you are entering at the right price, with a good likelihood that the price will move in your favor.

The Setup of a Short-Term Trade

For the short-term trade to be successful, you need to research several key factors that will influence the short-term movement in the right direction.

First, it's crucial that the overall market is moving in the same direction as the stock you are considering for a short-term investment. When the market is on your side, you are much more likely to see your chosen stock perform favorably.

So, if you're looking to buy a call on stock ABC and the fundamentals look in your favor, but the market is currently in pullback mode, it will be harder for you to realize the potential you're expecting. One of the best ways to do that is to read the technical charts and understand the indicators, which can help you determine the current direction of the market and what its next moves will likely be.

Following that, it's essential for short-term forecasts to be backed by a fundamental catalyst within the company to ensure progress. Keep an eye out for earnings revisions, as analysts frequently adjust their expectations for individual stock earnings, influencing stock price movements accordingly. A stock experiencing a positive earnings estimate revision will generally see its price trend upward in the days that follow.

Also, look for new product launches. If the company is planning on unveiling a new product, the market will adjust its price if the new product will add to the bottom line of earnings.

After mastering chart reading and consistently predicting the next movement, we can redefine the nature of the transaction. It shifts from being mere speculation to something more substantial. However, it wouldn't strictly qualify as an investment either. Thus, we can label it a business transaction. In business, engaging in short-term buying and selling to generate profits is common. When executed professionally, short-term trading—backed by effective preparation and money management—qualifies as a business transaction rather than just speculation.

This is a crucial differentiation that must not be ignored. Engaging in pure speculation with your hard-earned wealth is not advisable. Whether your wealth comes from an inheritance or lottery winnings, speculation is not a viable method for growing it.

If you've done your homework properly and have gained experience in understanding the movement of a business, you can predict the direction of a business or stock in the next few months based on several points of data. This is no longer the realm of speculation.

The Long Call - Give Yourself Extra Room

Once you have done all your homework properly, you know that the stock is heading in the right direction on the chart and that the market is similarly heading upward. You also have the proper catalyst of earnings revisions, etc., in place. The long call is perhaps the best way to proceed. The next hurdle is picking a strike price and expiration date.

Say stock ABC is trading at $100, and your analysis indicates it could reach $115 within the next month. A safer approach is to purchase the $100 strike option with an expiration date two or three months away. You might consider opting for the shorter-term call due to its lower premium, questioning the need for additional duration. After all, it's akin to paying for more insurance than you need. However, buying the extra month can be beneficial, as the slower time decay provides a buffer if your expectations don't materialize as anticipated.

The Long Put

Similar to a long call, but in the opposite direction, the long put strategy allows you to profit from a declining stock. Just as a long call serves in lieu of owning the stock itself, a long put serves in lieu of shorting the underlying stock. If you short the stock, you profit when the stock price falls; likewise, being long the put will yield a similar return.

However, there is a critical difference between shorting the actual stock and being long the put. If you short a stock expecting it to decline but it rises instead, your losses can be extreme. For example, if you short stock DEF at $100, expecting it to drop to $50, but it climbs to $150, you would lose $50 per share. If you shorted 1,000 shares, you would incur a loss of $50,000. On the other hand, if you bought a long put at $100, expecting it to decrease to $50, you likely paid around $10 per share for this put position, with a two-month expiration. If the stock drops to $50 as expected, you will gain $40 per share. However, if the stock rises to $150, you would only lose the $10 you paid for the put.

The long put strategy is most effective when the overall market appears gloomy. You identify one or two stocks that seem to be performing worse than the broader market due to negative news and troubling expectations.

The Covered Call

A **covered call** is an options strategy in which an investor owns shares of a stock and simultaneously sells a call option on those shares. This dual approach allows the investor to generate income from the option premium received while simultaneously limiting their potential upside on the stock.

The strategy works as follows: if the stock's market price remains below the strike price of the sold call option at expiration, the investor retains ownership of the stock along with the collected premium, effectively enhancing their income without risking the sale of the shares. However, if the stock's price increases above the strike price, the shares may be called away, meaning the investor must sell them at that predetermined strike price. This scenario results in profits being capped at the strike price plus the premium received, thereby limiting potential gains compared to if they held the stock without a covered call strategy.

Benefits of Covered Calls:

1. **Income Generation**: This approach creates income in flat or slightly bullish markets by taking advantage of the option premium, making it especially appealing during periods of market consolidation.

2. **Risk Mitigation**: Premium income acts as a buffer against potential losses, offering some protection against falls in stock prices.

3. **Improved Returns**: Covered calls can enhance overall investment returns for long-term investors, allowing them to earn premiums consistently while still holding onto their stocks.

Contrasting the Covered Call Strategy with Buying a Call:

In contrast to a covered call, buying a call option means acquiring the right to purchase a stock at a specific strike price within a designated timeframe, all without initially owning the shares. This strategy offers unlimited upside potential if the stock's price rises significantly, but it entails the risk of losing the entire premium paid for the option if the stock fails to surpass the strike price before expiration.

In essence, purchasing a call option can yield substantial returns in a robust, bullish market, but comes at the risk of losing the entire amount of the call option if your thesis doesn't go as planned and the stock remains stagnant. In contrast, covered calls offer a safer approach for investors prioritizing income or desiring a buffer in case the stock doesn't perform as expected.

The covered call strategy is all about lowering your risk exposure by getting income right off the bat at the entry of a stock position. This strategic balance of risk and reward enhances portfolio performance, especially amid uncertain market conditions.

Example: ALGN (Align Technology Inc) is trading for $182.54. Suppose you're bullish about the prospects of the company and expect the price to go up in the coming year and a half to two years. You are also cognizant of the competition ALGN has been facing, along with other market conditions, making you hesitant to buy at the current price unless you have a built-in cushion to help soften the volatility that may come up in the next little while.

You may want to set up a covered call position as follows:

1. Buy the stock for $182.54.
2. Sell the call at the strike price of $240 with an expiration date 19 months out into the future, thereby receiving $25.55 today.

The net of the two transactions is that your cost for the position will be lowered to $156.99. Calculated by subtracting the call option price from the stock price.

Now, at maturity, one of several things can happen. Let's break down two general scenarios:

Scenario #1: The stock price is at or above the strike price of $240. In this case, the stock will be called away from you and the buyer will pay you $240 per share. Your return on investment will be $83.01 per share or 52.9%. Calculated by dividing the return of $83.01 by the initial investment cost, $156.99.

In this case, the stock may have only climbed 31.5% to $240 from the initial price of $182.54, but you have made 52.9% because your cost base was lower than the initial stock price.

Scenario #2: The stock is below the strike price at maturity. You get to keep the stock, and you can sell a new covered call against it for further income. Each time you sell a new covered call, you are effectively lowering your cost base. By lowering your cost base, you're also lowering your risk exposure.

ALGN **$182.54** ▲$3.30 Real-time ⊘

EQUITY:
Long 600 shares at $182.54

EXPIRATION: 1.7y

May		Jun			Jul	Sep	Oct	Jan '26	Mar	Jun	Dec	Jan '27
23	30	6	13	20	27	18	19	17	16	20	18	18	15

STRIKE:

ALGN

75 90 100 110 120 130 140 150 160 170 180 190 200 220 240 260 280 300 320 340 360 380

240C ▲

NET CREDIT: ≡ $15,330	MAX LOSS: $94,194	MAX PROFIT: ↗ $49,806	CHANCE OF PROFIT: 📈 60%	BREAKEVEN: ↑ Above $156.99 (-14%)

		May 20	Jun 23	Jul 23	Aug 25	Oct 29	Nov 2	Dec 4	Jan '26 9	Feb 9	Mar 13	Apr 19	May 21	Jun 25	Jul 29	Sep 3	Oct 6	Nov 9	Dec 14	Jan '2 15
$289	98%	25%	26%	27%	27%	28%	30%	31%	32%	34%	35%	37%	38%	40%	42%	43%	45%	47%	50%	52%	53%
$279	93%	23%	24%	26%	26%	27%	28%	29%	31%	32%	34%	35%	37%	38%	40%	42%	44%	46%	49%	51%	53%
$270	49%	22%	23%	24%	24%	25%	27%	28%	29%	31%	32%	34%	35%	37%	39%	41%	43%	45%	48%	51%	53%
$260	42%	20%	21%	22%	22%	24%	25%	26%	27%	29%	30%	32%	33%	35%	37%	39%	41%	43%	46%	49%	53%
$250	37%	18%	19%	20%	20%	22%	23%	24%	25%	27%	28%	30%	31%	33%	35%	37%	39%	41%	44%	48%	53%
$241	30%	16%	17%	18%	18%	20%	21%	22%	23%	25%	26%	28%	29%	31%	33%	34%	37%	39%	42%	45%	53%
$231	27%	14%	15%	15%	16%	17%	18%	20%	21%	22%	24%	25%	27%	28%	30%	32%	34%	36%	39%	42%	47%
$221	21%	11%	13%	13%	14%	15%	16%	17%	18%	19%	21%	22%	24%	25%	27%	28%	30%	32%	35%	38%	41%
$212	16%	8.1%	10%	11%	11%	12%	13%	14%	16%	17%	18%	19%	21%	22%	24%	25%	27%	29%	31%	33%	35%
$202	11%	6.2%	7.1%	8%	8.1%	9.1%	10%	11%	12%	13%	15%	16%	17%	18%	20%	21%	23%	24%	26%	28%	29%
$192	5.2%	3.1%	4%	4.8%	4.9%	5.9%	6.8%	7.8%	8.8%	9.8%	11%	12%	13%	14%	16%	17%	18%	20%	21%	22%	22%
$183	0.3%	0.1%	0.9%	1.7%	1.8%	2.7%	3.6%	4.5%	5.4%	6.4%	7.4%	8.4%	9.4%	10%	12%	13%	14%	15%	16%	16%	17%
$173	-5.2%	-3.5%	-2.7%	-2%	-2%	-1.1%	-0.3%	0.5%	1.4%	2.2%	3.1%	4%	4.9%	5.8%	6.7%	7.6%	8.4%	9.2%	9.8%	10%	10%
$163	-10%	-7.3%	-6.6%	-6%	-5.9%	-5.2%	-4.5%	-3.7%	-3%	-2.3%	-1.5%	-0.7%	0%	0.8%	1.5%	2.2%	2.8%	3.3%	3.7%	3.8%	3.8%
$153	-16%	-11%	-11%	-10%	-10%	-9.6%	-8.9%	-8.3%	-7.8%	-7%	-6.4%	-5.8%	-5.2%	-4.6%	-4%	-3.5%	-3.1%	-2.8%	-2.8%	-2.5%	-2.5%
$144	-21%	-15%	-15%	-14%	-14%	-14%	-13%	-13%	-12%	-12%	-11%	-11%	-10%	-9.6%	-9.2%	-8.9%	-8.6%	-8.4%	-8.3%	-8.3%	-8.3%
$134	-27%	-20%	-20%	-19%	-19%	-19%	-18%	-18%	-17%	-17%	-16%	-16%	-16%	-15%	-15%	-15%	-15%	-15%	-15%	-15%	-15%
$124	-32%	-25%	-25%	-24%	-24%	-24%	-23%	-23%	-23%	-22%	-22%	-22%	-22%	-21%	-21%	-21%	-21%	-21%	-21%	-21%	-21%
$115	-37%	-30%	-29%	-29%	-29%	-29%	-28%	-28%	-28%	-28%	-27%	-27%	-27%	-27%	-27%	-27%	-27%	-27%	-27%	-27%	-27%
$105	-43%	-35%	-35%	-35%	-35%	-34%	-34%	-34%	-34%	-34%	-34%	-33%	-33%	-33%	-33%	-33%	-33%	-33%	-33%	-33%	-33%
$95	-48%	-41%	-41%	-40%	-40%	-40%	-40%	-40%	-40%	-40%	-40%	-40%	-40%	-40%	-40%	-39%	-39%	-39%	-39%	-39%	-39%
$80	-53%	-46%	-46%	-46%	-46%	-46%	-46%	-45%	-45%	-45%	-45%	-45%	-45%	-45%	-45%	-45%	-45%	-45%	-45%	-45%	-45%
$76	-58%	-52%	-52%	-52%	-52%	-52%	-52%	-52%	-52%	-52%	-52%	-52%	-52%	-52%	-52%	-52%	-52%	-52%	-52%	-52%	-52%

Debit Call Spread

A **debit call spread** is an investment strategy used when someone thinks a stock's price will go up moderately. It works by **buying a call option** (which gives the right to buy the stock) at a lower price and **selling another call option** at a higher price, both of which have the same expiration date. The money received from selling the higher-priced call helps reduce the cost of buying the lower-priced call. This makes the strategy less **expensive than simply buying one call option, yet** it still lets the investor make a profit if the stock price increases.

Benefits:

Lower cost and **risk** – The premium is cheaper than a standalone call option.

Defined risk and **reward** – The maximum loss is equivalent to the premium paid, while the maximum profit is the difference between the strike prices minus the premium.

Benefits in moderate uptrends – This strategy performs well with moderate price rises, not requiring a large increase.

Enhanced chances of success—Profit potential is available even with minimal stock movement, giving this strategy a competitive edge.

This strategy is ideal for investors who want **controlled risk** while benefiting from an expected stock price increase. It provides a balanced risk-reward approach compared to outright call buying.

Jesse Livermore

When it comes to potentially speculative instruments, I must emphasize the significant dangers and pitfalls that can emerge. Jesse Livermore, one of the most renowned traders in history, rose from modest beginnings to great wealth, only to experience numerous losses. Born in 1877, he began trading as a teenager, where he learned to interpret market patterns in bucket shops (illegal betting establishments for stocks). His keen instincts earned him a considerable fortune but also led to his ban from many of these shops.

He later transitioned to Wall Street, where he amassed millions by shorting stocks during the crashes of 1907 and 1929. His most notable achievement occurred in 1929, when he successfully bet against the market just before the onset of the Great Depression, pocketing $100 million (about $1.7 billion today).

Nevertheless, Livermore's narrative is marked by significant ups and downs. Despite his exceptional talent, he suffered catastrophic losses due to overleveraging and emotionally driven trading. By the late 1930s, he found himself bankrupt.

Tragically, Livermore's life ended in suicide in 1940. Despite this, his insights into market psychology, risk management, and trend following are still considered legendary. His book, *Reminiscences of a Stock Operator*, remains an essential reading for traders.

At one time, Livermore was among the richest people in the world; however, at the time of his suicide, his liabilities exceeded his assets.

Jesse Livermore's story is one of legendary highs and crushing lows. Livermore is often recognized as a pioneer of day trading, embodying the power—and perils—of speculation. His life was a rollercoaster of incredible triumphs and devastating losses, and his legacy serves as a cautionary tale more than a source of inspiration—a blueprint for what not to do.

His narrative poignantly reminds us that discipline and emotional control are just as vital as a strategy for achieving success in trading.

The journey from rags to riches and back to rags again, filled with heartache, evokes the metaphor of the hare and the tortoise. It's hard not to appreciate the value of being a content tortoise, making steady progress towards a rewarding destination after a long journey, rather than being a despondent hare who, despite touching the stars, ultimately falls into despair.

Just recently, we heard in the news of the story of an RBC lawsuit related to a young client of 20-something years old, who went from less than $100K to over $400 million in a few short years by trading Tesla options and then lost it all.

Now, Jesse was a sophisticated speculator, and this guy in his 20s claimed to have limited knowledge, stating he didn't really understand his risks.

So, while their stories differ, there's a powerful lesson that links them: LEVERAGE.

When used wisely, leverage can fuel remarkable success, but it's a sharp, double-edged sword that can also lead to rapid, catastrophic losses if misused.

Certainly, the excitement and attraction of the stock market resemble aggressive mimicry, enticing in a subtle yet clever manner. This allure can be even more potent in the options market because of its high leverage and rapid pace. If not managed carefully, this risky asset can result in complete devastation.

How to Avoid this Wreckage by Putting in the Right Checks and Balances

Leverage isn't just a financial tool; it can become an emotional burden. When things go right, it feels exhilarating. But when they go wrong, the weight of mounting losses and financial stress can be overwhelming. The losses don't just drain bank accounts—they drain energy, confidence, and, at times, hope.

Manage Leverage Responsibly

Understand Your Risk – Leverage amplifies both gains and losses. Ask yourself: are you really comfortable with the potential downsides?

Have a Safety Net – Avoid going "all in" with borrowed money. Keep cash reserves and create a margin of safety for unexpected developments.

Focus on Long-Term Goals – Leveraging for short-term gains can lead to rash decisions. Consider leverage only when it fits a well-thought-out, long-term strategy.

Continuous Learning – Markets change, and so should your knowledge. Stay updated about the assets you're investing in and the risks involved with leverage.

Leverage can be a powerful ally or a risky foe—it all depends on how well you understand and manage it.

A strong investment mindset prioritizes longevity over fleeting gains. Stay disciplined, stay informed, and be cautious when using leverage.

The Emotional Side

Investing involves more than just numbers; it encompasses our dreams, relationships, mental health, and sometimes even our identity. For individuals like Livermore, the emotional burden of significant financial losses can seem inescapable.

Here are key takeaways from these stories:

1. Prioritize Mental Wellbeing – Financial stress can be intense. Stay aware of your mental health and don't hesitate to reach out for help when necessary.

2. Know Your Limits – Be aware of how leverage affects you, both financially and emotionally. If a potential loss feels too overwhelming, it's likely too risky to pursue.

3. Have a Strong Support System – Navigating financial highs and lows is more manageable with friends, family, or mentors by your side. Don't face these struggles alone.

4. Financial Success Doesn't Define You—Market gains and losses are merely numbers. True wealth encompasses good health, meaningful relationships, and inner peace of mind.

Sustainable investing requires both financial and emotional resilience. Investing is a journey, not a sprint.

CHAPTER #9

Allocation and Diversification

"Diversification may preserve wealth, but concentration builds wealth."

— Warren Buffett

This chapter may be the most important one in terms of creating a happy, smooth ride with your investments. The ideas shared here on allocation and diversification are so critical, they can make all the difference between success and failure.

Until now, we have laid out many different and diverse investment ideas. Each with its own unique characteristics. Each with its own set of pros and cons. And each will relate to economic advances or contractions in a different way.

While each investment strategy is expected to yield positive returns over the next 10 to 20 years, and potentially even over the next 5 to 7 years, there will likely be notable variances in their performance within the next 2 to 4 years. Some strategies may underperform, while others are likely to perform adequately.

Stocks are at the top of the list of this variation of returns.

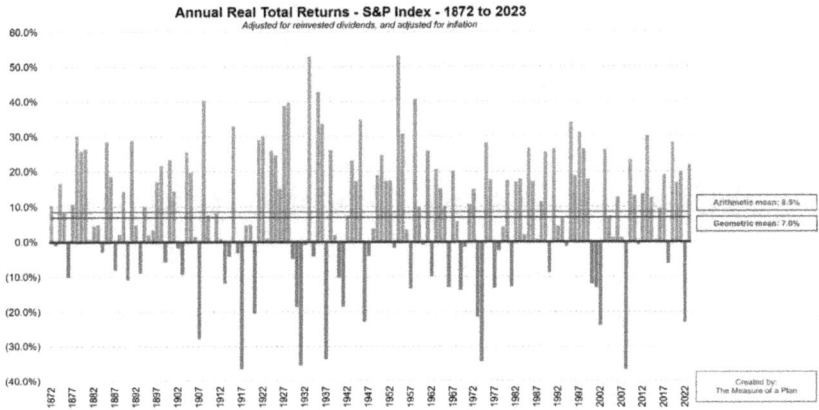

Annual Real Total Returns - S&P Index - 1872 to 2023
Adjusted for reinvested dividends, and adjusted for inflation

However, variations of returns are not proprietary to stocks. Bonds also have a wide range of returns throughout the last decade.

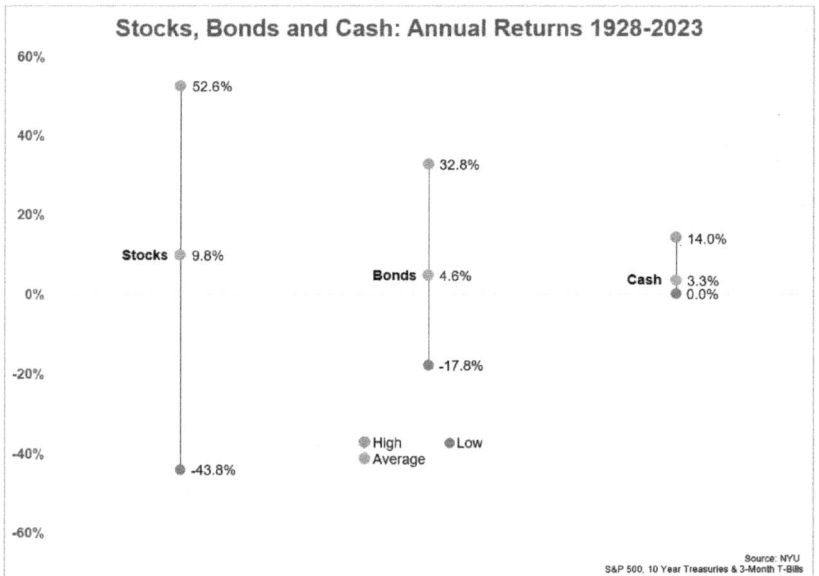

Stocks, Bonds and Cash: Annual Returns 1928-2023

And so does almost any other investment that isn't a GIC or similar guaranteed holding. There will be variations in return from year to year. And there should be.

In fact, one of the things you should look out for as a red flag is an investment that has performed a steady return of, say, 10% year in and year out. Just like our heartbeat, our economy is constantly fluctuating. As you can see on an electrocardiogram, the worst thing is a steady line, which would set alarms off in a medical clinic or hospital ward. Similarly, the economy is constantly fluctuating, and any investment related to economic performance will fluctuate in its return behavior.

So this is where diversification helps. Proper diversification is not accomplished through investing in different companies. Yes, this will help mitigate certain risks related directly to the management of a particular company. But that's not going to mitigate against risks related to the sector as a whole. And it will certainly not mitigate the risks of economic fluctuations.

To mitigate the risks of economic variances, we need to create diverse assets that behave differently in response to economic news.

This means that a portfolio with diverse asset class types will be much better able to withstand downturns. The portfolio as a whole will fluctuate much less than any individual segment.

A simple example is stocks vs. bonds. When the stock market pulls back 30% due to an economic contraction, the investment-grade bond market as a whole will hold its value and even go up nicely due to the simultaneous lowering of interest rates that comes with economic turbulence.

Another prevalent example I use when illustrating this idea to clients and implementing it in their portfolios is real estate rental units. When the economy contracts and, if it gets really ugly, people lose their jobs, the real estate rental market generally holds its ground. This is because there will continue to be demand for rental units, and the price of rent will steadily increase.

We saw this in the recent difficulty of COVID. Even while people were being laid off for a certain period of time, our rental units allocation performed very well. The demand for rentals increased as people were selling their homes and downsizing to rental units due to their economic squeeze. Anyone who was in a rental unit didn't want to let go as the market price of rent had increased significantly, and their rent was stabilized at a rate 20 percent below current market rental prices.

Negative Correlation

The investment term for this type of diversification into different asset classes is called negative correlation. In true negative correlation, one investment will rise while the other falls. We aren't looking for that. What we are really looking for is diverse investments that will all rise over time, but their relationship with the risks of the economy are not related. Over a twenty-year period, both the stock market and the bond market will likely perform according to its long-term average historic returns. But in any given year when the stock markets are troublesome, the bond market will compensate. Similarly, the rental units previously described will surely produce a good return over the next twenty years, but this investment has its own set of unique economic risks. Those risks will likely not show up in the same years the economy is in trouble.

By including these diverse asset classes in a portfolio, we can smooth out the fluctuations of the portfolio as a whole.

Two Opposing Opinions About Diversification.

There is a fascinating dispute about stock diversification.

The first viewpoint is widely recognized among market participants, analysts, and investors as the 'efficient market hypothesis.' To simplify, this hypothesis suggests that because the stock market operates efficiently, attempting to surpass the market through individual stock selection is ineffective. Instead, it is more advantageous to invest in index funds that encompass the entire market.

At the other extreme of this position are people like Warren Buffett and Charlie Munger, who have had enormous continuous success outperforming the market by choosing companies they deem good value, trading below the intrinsic value of the company, and then holding them until the stock market price rises above the deemed intrinsic value.

Their ability to continuously outperform the market certainly supports that the market is not perfectly efficient. With an intelligently trained eye, the professional investor can find holdings and create a portfolio that can outperform the market.

As a by-product of their ability to choose companies that will outperform the market, Buffett and Munger have a high concentration of stock investments. As can be seen from the following chart, their top 8 stocks have more than 65% of the portfolio concentration as of late 2024.

Largest Berkshire Stock Holdings as of Nov 2024

	Symbol	Holdings	Stake	Mkt price	Value	Pct of portfolio
TOTAL					$298,248,009,057	100.0%
Apple Inc	AAPL	300,000,000	2.0%	$229.87	$68,961,000,000	23.1%
American Express Company	AXP	151,610,700	21.5%	$301.30	$45,680,303,910	15.3%
Bank of America Corp	BAC	766,305,462	9.99%	$47.00	$36,016,356,714	12.1%
Coca-Cola Co	KO	400,000,000	9.3%	$63.92	$25,568,000,000	8.6%
Chevron Corp	CVX	118,610,534	6.6%	$162.36	$19,257,606,300	6.5%
Occidental Petroleum Corp	OXY	255,281,524	27.2%	$51.93	$13,256,769,541	4.4%
Moody's Corp	MCO	24,669,778	13.6%	$480.66	$11,857,775,493	4.0%
Kraft Heinz Co	KHC	325,634,818	26.9%	$31.81	$10,358,443,561	3.5%

However, it is important to note and understand three main advantages of Munger and Buffet.

1. They are either on the board and advise the companies they invest heavily in or are in close contact with the CEO and other top executives of those companies. Which leads to advantage #2.

2. They are much more confident about allocating money because they know there will be no significant internal surprises.

3. As they have written, they can withstand a 50% drop in value and endure the economic difficulties. They have such confidence in the fundamental qualities of the businesses they invest in that they will not sell out due to price fluctuations.

They usually won't have these advantages at the outset of allocating money to these companies. So, initially, they would solely rely on the quarterly and annual statements that the companies produce. But they have become exceptionally skilled at knowing how to interpret not only what is written in those statements but, more importantly, how to read between the lines of what isn't clearly stated. I once heard Buffett say (loosely quoting) that he reads as much information about a specific subject as possible and then reflects on that information to create a picture of the subject in a way that provides clarity beyond the written word.

If you have these advantages in a company or industry, then you should also be concentrated and over-allocate to the areas you completely understand once doing your due diligence. Otherwise, diversification is key.

In general, I like to tell clients to be invested where they feel comfortable, confident, and have conviction.

But the key is not just to be confident and have conviction when the investment is performing well. That's no skill. The key is to have done so much research and feel so good about a particular company or investment holding that no matter what happens in the coming years, you will hold through thick and thin.

I remember a risk-averse client who once told me that he wanted to invest in the S&P 500 because he believed the overall US economy could do no wrong. After about six months, when the US economy was underperforming, that client sold out of the S&P 500. What happened here? This reflects how many amateur investors behave. They don't perform their due diligence and lack substantial data to support their thesis. Typically, they base their investments on hearsay, whether from a social club or an online forum. However, they often neglect to examine the company's statements firsthand. In that client's case, even with the benefits of being diversified across the largest and most reputable 500 publicly traded companies in the US, he wanted to exit because he hadn't grounded his investment in independent research to establish sufficient conviction.

Getting back to the dispute over market efficiency and diversification, my approach has been to take a little of both sides of the argument. On one hand, I believe diversification of asset classes is critically important to creating an optimal risk/reward portfolio. At the same time, within any particular asset class, I will do significant research to find the best company or holding in that sector or asset class, not necessarily holding the entire asset class.

Absolute Return vs. Risk/Reward Return

One thing investors need to understand and decide while creating their portfolio of diverse investments is the difference between getting the best absolute returns and getting the best return for a certain amount of risk.

What is your objective? Do you want to get the highest possible return that can be achieved or do you want to get the best return while keeping within a particular bracket of risk exposure?

What is Risk?

In order to get clarity on "risk," let's first define the word risk. There are many different ways to view risk. Risk has different meanings in different scenarios.

In the investment realm, one common way the world interprets risk is as the possibility of an investment outcome being different from what was anticipated.

If you invested $1 million expecting it to grow to $2 million in 10 years, and it ends up being $1.5 million after that period, this outcome would differ and could lead to unintended consequences. For instance, if you planned to purchase a specific property with $2 million, you may now need to wait longer for that purchase. Or, if you were counting on retiring with $2 million in ten years, you would only have 75% of the expected amount. This could be a serious issue, as you would only have enough to cover 75% of your intended retirement. You might have to cancel all the enjoyable activities, heaven forbid.

OK, now that we have clarity on the definition of risk, let's return to the previous question.

Are you looking to achieve the highest possible return or just the best return within a particular comfort zone of risk that you are willing to take?

When asked this way, the answer is clear. No one should take on unnecessary risk exposure; even if you might get compensated for that higher risk, you might also not. There's a good chance you end up worse off because of that unwarranted extra risk you took on. Remember, higher risk means a higher chance your objectives and plans don't pan out.

This is why there is no good cookie-cutter solution for an investment portfolio. Because each individual wants to get the best return for the amount of risk they are willing to undertake. And since each person is unique with what risk they are willing to take, the optimal investment portfolio will differ accordingly.

Buffet and Munger were perfectly fine with their investments going down on paper 50% in any given year. They would have been fine money-wise. This wouldn't affect them at all in terms of their ability to live comfortably for the rest of their lives. Additionally, they understand the system so well and have such conviction in what they have invested that they won't sell out of the investments just because they're down temporarily. They will hold through thick and thin, knowing that this is the economy as a whole and all will work out over time.

If you are in the same position as them, then great. There may not be any need to create a negative correlation within your portfolio, and you can invest in all stocks for the absolute best return. At the end of the day, you have done your research and are confident that the companies you've invested in will be fine even in the downturn of the economy. So, the drop is only on paper and temporary. It will climb back up sooner or later.

That is not doable for the average person. That strategy doesn't work for most people who have not built an Olympic athletic muscle of emotional intelligence around the stock market and its ins and outs.

The advantage of negative correlation with different risk assets that all have the objective of growth but differ in their risk exposures is that it creates a buffer of protection like an "airbag" when the market "crashes" 30% every couple of years.

You may not get the highest absolute return, but the lower risk will keep you "alive" and invested, and you will not feel the need to sell the entire portfolio at the worst time and run for the hills. This is the advantage of thinking in terms of risk/reward as opposed to absolute return.

Diversify to Retain Peace of Mind

Allocation percentages of each asset class or strategy are based on each individual's investment time horizon, prior experience, and future goals with the money.

An allocation to any one asset class or investment holding should not create excitement, either positive or negative. The key is to remain objective throughout the investment's lifecycle and not let emotions cloud your mind.

It's interesting to see, and I see this repeatedly in my practice. Whenever clients get emotional and excited about an investment's capabilities on the way up, they likely get worried when it underperforms. Our job is to remain rational in our decision-making. We want our investments to be solely based on sound research. Same for the time of selling. The sale of the security should not be based on the negative sentiments currently brewing in the markets. Remember the parable of Mr. Market from Ben Graham in Chapter 4. We are meant to take advantage of the bi-polar sentiments of the market and not be dragged into their traps.

Proper diversification and allocating the right amount to each holding allows us to remain level-headed and endure market swings. Since each holding represents a predetermined portion of our wealth, we will not be worked up.

CHAPTER 10

Why Use An Advisor

"Obstacles don't have to stop you. If you run into a wall, don't turn around and give up. Figure out how to climb it, go through it, or work around it."

– Michael Jordan

"A good coach will make his players see what they can be rather than what they are."

– Ara Parasheghian

I recently read a fascinating interview of David Magerman, a top data scientist who joined the famous hedge fund Renaissance Technologies in 1995.

Renaissance Technologies is known as the best hedge fund in history, with an average annual after-fee return of 39% between 1988 and 2018.

The uniqueness of Renaissance is that they don't hire Wall Street-style investment managers. They are solely interested in computer scientists, mathematicians and physicists to be part of their staff. They adopted Artificial Intelligence in the earliest stages of computers, and they made it extremely profitable.

When David Magerman joined Renaissance as a junior programmer, he described being placed in a small department of the hedge fund that dealt with equities markets.

At the time, the equities division accounted for 5% of the company's capital, but it was actually losing a lot of money year after year. The company compensated for this loss by doing well in its other divisions, such as currency exchange, bonds, and commodities.

David rose through the ranks quickly and was responsible for turning the equities division into a profitable one that grew bigger than several other divisions over the coming years. His work contributed to the fund's growth by billions.

David left the fund in 2017 with a 10-year non-compete agreement that prohibits him from creating anything similar until 2027.

What struck me most about the article was when, at one point, the interviewer asked David if he currently invests in the stock market, to which David responded, "The stock market is rigged against the little people. I don't invest in it." This anecdote was mind-blowing to me.

Here is a person who was instrumental in turning a failing division of an extremely successful hedge fund into one of the most successful divisions and contributing billions to its bottom line. However, he doesn't trust his ability to understand the market's fundamentals. He doesn't want to rely on his ability to pick a stock based on its fundamentals. And he prefers to stay away from the stock market?!

He added: "If I were doing quantitative modeling, I might."

In other words, his entire exposure to equities was about the AI of the computer, which provided instructions on what to buy and sell and then actually did the buying and selling on its own. Human interaction was only about making a computer program that would do its work well. So, David, the human, never gained trust in the long-term success and viability of the stock market.

The lesson? Stay in your lane.

Know what you're good at. You likely have had success in your business and personal life. Do more of that which you are great at.

If you don't intend to invest as a professional and dedicate your heart and soul to it, it will likely not work out well.

I'm not saying you shouldn't try new skills. Yes, I love learning new skills. One Sunday, I spent several hours changing a broken bathroom faucet. I had the plumber on call just in case it didn't work out. And it was a bit of a struggle. It took perseverance, and when it was done, it felt amazing.

But the stakes were low. I wasn't doing anything that could flood the entire floor and create havoc.

When you're dealing with your retirement nest egg, it is far better to have a good advisor help you out.

The Value of an Investment Coach or Advisor: Why Expertise and Discipline Matter

Throughout this book, we've explored various investment strategies, from diversification to setting up different types of holdings. These are essential foundations for building a solid portfolio. However, as you transition into the next phase of your financial journey—whether you're approaching retirement or navigating life post-retirement—there's one critical element that we need to address: the importance of having a coach or advisor to guide you.

For individuals who have amassed significant wealth—say $2 million or more—the stakes are too high to risk your financial future on poorly researched ideas or emotional decision-making. At this stage in life, every decision must be made with the utmost care and foresight. And this is where the expertise of a professional investment advisor or coach becomes invaluable.

Why DIY Investing May Not Be Enough

Some people at this stage enjoy the process of selecting investments themselves. They feel confident in their ability to make sound decisions, and for these individuals, managing a portion of their wealth in a self-directed account can be both educational and enjoyable. Whether they're watching financial programs, researching online, or seeking insights from investment gurus, the process can provide intellectual stimulation and a sense of control.

But here's the truth: the bulk of your wealth should be managed by a professional.

Why? Because investing isn't just about knowledge or even technical skill—it's about emotional discipline. Most investors, even those with considerable knowledge, fall victim to the twin pitfalls of greed and fear:

- **Greed:** During market highs, the euphoria of rising prices entices investors to buy at inflated levels, chasing returns that have already been realized.

- **Fear:** During market downturns, panic sets in, prompting many to sell at a loss to "cut their losses," often at the worst possible time.

This emotional cycle is one of the biggest reasons why the average investor underperforms the very funds they invest in. Consider this well-known statistic: even in funds managed by top-performing fund managers, with returns averaging 25% annually over 20 years, the average investor in those funds achieved net-zero returns. The culprit? Emotional decision-making—buying high and selling low.

The Emotional Edge of a Professional

A seasoned advisor offers more than technical expertise—they provide a buffer against emotional missteps. They are one step removed from your natural emotional attachment to your money. This allows them to make rational decisions based on data, trends, and a long-term perspective, rather than being swayed by market noise.

When you work with an advisor, you're not just hiring someone to manage your portfolio; you're gaining a partner who:

1. **Sees the Bigger Picture**: Advisors help you stay focused on long-term goals, even when short-term volatility feels overwhelming.

2. **Implements Proven Strategies**: Professionals can access tools, insights, and strategies that the average investor might not.

3. **Provides Accountability**: They ensure you stick to your investment plan, preventing impulsive decisions that could derail your financial future.

Balancing Autonomy with Expertise

If you enjoy managing investments and have the time and inclination to do so, that's fantastic. But it's essential to strike a balance. One strategy is to allocate a small percentage of your portfolio—say 5–10%—to a self-directed account. This allows you to experiment, learn, and engage in the investment process without jeopardizing your financial security.

For the bulk of your portfolio, entrusting it to a professional ensures that your wealth is safeguarded and optimized. Think of this as separating your "play money" from your "serious money."

Exploring Prop Trading as an Alternative

Prop trading accounts are another intriguing option for those who want to trade and hone their skills actively.

Here's how it works:

1. **Subscription Model**: You pay a small fee—typically between $50 and $300 per month—to access a trading account funded by the firm. Initially, this is a simulated account to test your skills.

2. **Performance Evaluation**: If you meet the firm's performance criteria, you can graduate to trading live accounts with real money provided by the firm.

3. **Risk Management**: The firm bears most of the financial risk, while you gain valuable experience trading more significant sums of money.

4. **High Payouts**: In some prop firms, you can keep up to 80-90% of the gains!

This approach offers several benefits:

- **Low Financial Risk**: Your only investment is the subscription fee, which is minimal compared to potential losses in a self-funded account.

- **Skill Development**: You can develop and refine your trading skills without risking your personal wealth.

- **Real-World Experience**: Trading with firm capital provides a more realistic and emotionally engaging experience than paper trading.

However, it's important to understand that prop trading isn't for everyone. It requires discipline, a willingness to learn, and the ability to handle the pressure of trading with firm-imposed guidelines.

The Role of Paper Trading

Before diving into prop trading, consider starting with paper trading. Many platforms offer simulated accounts where you can practice trading with "monopoly money." While this is a valuable way to learn the mechanics of trading, it has limitations.

The biggest drawback? There's no emotional attachment to paper money. Without the psychological pressure of real financial stakes, it's impossible to fully replicate the experience of live trading. This is why prop trading, with its low-risk entry point, can be a better option for those looking to take their skills to the next level.

The Bottom Line: Protecting Your Wealth

Whether you choose to dabble in self-directed investing, explore prop trading, or stick to a fully managed portfolio, one thing remains clear: your serious money should not be left to chance.

Professional advisors bring an emotional detachment and level of expertise that is invaluable for preserving and growing your wealth. They help you avoid the common pitfalls of emotional investing, provide access to advanced tools and strategies, and ensure that your financial plan aligns with your long-term goals.

Investing can be an exciting and rewarding hobby, especially for retirees with time to dedicate to learning and analysis. But remember: the purpose of investing is to secure your financial future—not to gamble it away. With the right balance of professional guidance and personal engagement, you can achieve both security and satisfaction in your investment journey.

Conclusion: Your Wealth, Your Why, Your Legacy

Congratulations on taking this important journey toward financial success and emotional well-being. By reading this book, you've embraced not just the practicalities of investing but also the deeper connections between money, emotions, and peace of mind. Your commitment to understanding these ideas sets the stage for a prosperous future filled with clarity and confidence.

As your portfolio grows beyond $2 to $3 million, the importance of a personalized investment strategy becomes undeniable. A well-crafted portfolio goes beyond the basics of stocks and bonds—it integrates alternative investments, diverse asset classes, and thoughtful planning tailored to your unique goals. With the proper guidance, emotional resilience, and disciplined decision-making, you can build a portfolio that not only grows but also brings you lasting peace of mind. No more sleepless nights over market swings. No more panicked reactions to sensational headlines.

Instead of locking away a large portion of your wealth in low-return investments for a false sense of security, you can achieve stability and growth with a custom portfolio aligned with your risk tolerance and objectives. This personalized approach can help you not just keep pace with inflation but potentially outpace it, maximizing your wealth while maintaining your comfort.

Now, the choice is yours: will your hard-earned nest egg merely maintain its value over time, or will it grow and thrive, taking full advantage of the opportunities available to you? Will you stick with outdated strategies, or will you embrace a diversified, tailored approach that opens doors to greater returns and genuine peace of mind? The difference is striking—both in your financial outcomes and in how you feel about the journey.

Finding Your "Why"

As we conclude, I want to leave you with a thought about your "why." You've likely heard about the importance of having a personal "why"—a reason that drives your decisions and actions. Many people believe their "why" is essential for navigating tough times, for keeping them grounded during obstacles and challenges. While this is true, I want to emphasize something equally important: your "why" matters just as much in good times, in moments of success.

Too often, when people achieve success, they lose sight of their original purpose. Consider those who enter politics with noble intentions—to serve the community, to bring positive change. Once they climb the ladder of success, however, they sometimes forget their ideals, consumed by the pursuit of power, status, and resources. The same can happen with wealth. Without a clear "why," it's easy to lose track of what truly matters.

Your "why" isn't just a guide through challenges; it's your compass in moments of triumph. What is your reason for building wealth? Is it your family, your loved ones, your desire to leave a legacy? Never lose sight of that.

A Parable of Purpose

Let me share a parable that illustrates this point.

A lioness, determined to provide for her cubs, was constantly on the hunt. Whenever her cubs sought her attention—yearning for affection, play, and connection—she would say, "Not now, little ones. I need to hunt. Stay here, and I'll return soon." And so, she would leave them, pouring her energy into becoming a skilled and successful hunter.

The cubs grew up strong and independent, learning to fend for themselves. But one day, the lioness, after achieving so much as a hunter, realized something was missing. She wanted to reconnect with her cubs, to nurture and bond with them. Yet, when she returned, she found they had grown distant, busy with their own lives. The time to build that connection had passed.

The lioness learned too late that while success is important, so are the relationships and connections that give life its meaning.

Your Wealth, Your Purpose

Wealth is more than numbers on a statement; it's about purpose and meaning. Many wealthy individuals struggle with fractured relationships, distrust, and a sense of emptiness. We've discussed "affluenza," the discontent that arises when wealth exists without a deeper purpose. True financial success is about more than growth—it's about aligning your wealth with your values, building stronger connections, and leaving a legacy of meaning.

So as you move forward, remember your "why." Let your investments serve not just your financial goals but also the things that matter most: your family, your dreams, and your legacy. Reach out to create a personalized investment portfolio that reflects not only your financial ambitions but also your vision for a meaningful and fulfilling life.

The choice is yours—prosper with purpose.

APPENDIX

Some readers may be wondering how recent economic events regarding tariffs impact investing. To provide more information on this topic, I've included as an appendix three newsletters I wrote to my clients on the subject. The March 28 and April 4 newsletters were written during the downturn, while the May 12 newsletter was written when the markets began to move upward. I hope these newsletters help you gain clarity on how this recent tariff saga impacts the markets.

CONSUMER SENTIMENT FALLING AS TRADE WARS CONTINUE TO BE A REALITY

March 28 2025

The March Michigan Consumer Sentiment number was reported today, and we see a significant drop, which was somewhat expected, though it did come a bit lower than anticipated.

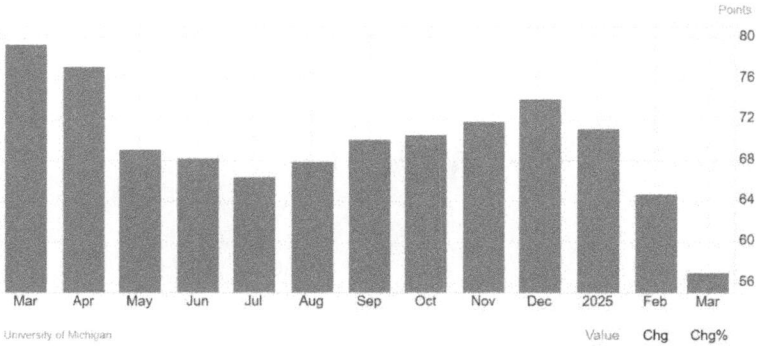

University of Michigan

The markets didn't like this at all and reacted with a 2% drop as of this afternoon.

This puts the US market at 9% off its February high. And confirms that the end of last week's market calm was just a breather before heading further down.

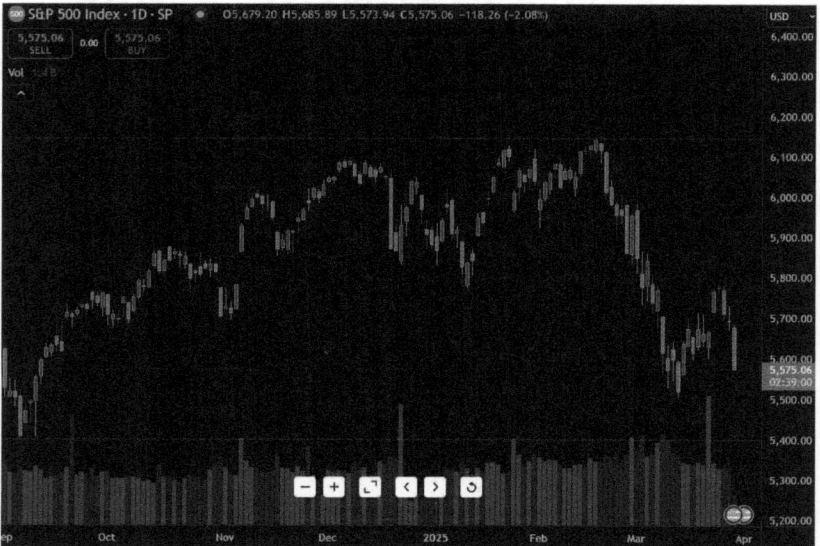

From experience, it is right after we turn up for a breather and then continue the downtrend, precisely when the news on every business station will begin recommending that everyone sell off their investment holdings.

I've seen this several times in my career. When the markets initially go down, everyone is calm, and the news doesn't panic. They say it's just a short-term correction. But as soon as the second leg down begins, that's when everyone gets worried and excited.

Since the beginning of the year, I have advocated a cautious approach to equities. I sold covered calls on positions to hedge exposure and advocated safe, steady positions as a basket of protection.

The right time to make big restructuring moves was in late December and early January, when the markets were overly optimistic. At year end, I went over all our larger positions and created a list, rating each holding. We sold those positions that came up overpriced, and on several others, we sold covered calls, as mentioned.

Now, while it will likely get worse before getting better, the best thing at this point is likely to hold off and wait for the buying opportunities that will come in the coming weeks or months.

Where are we going from here?

I think we are currently halfway off the high and will likely hit close to the lower 5000 mark on the SP500 sometime in the coming months. This also happens to coincide with the trend that began in March 2020, following the purple line in the chart below.

Do I know this with certainty? Absolutely not. And that's why I'm not recommending anyone liquidate positions at this point.

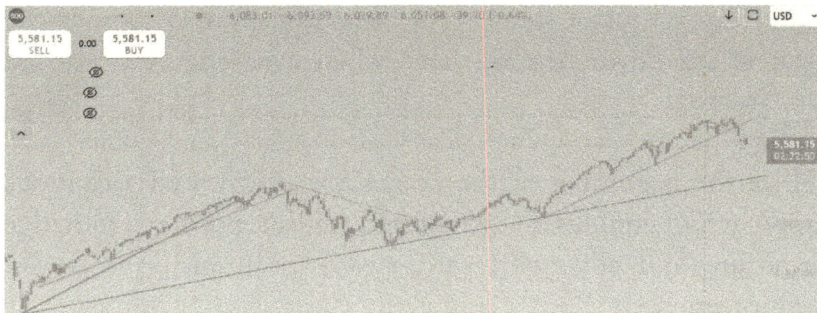

I look at it more like sitting in a dentist's chair. While the drilling is a bit painful, the knowledge that we're halfway done with the pain is a bit soothing.

What makes me think that we are heading to the 5000 mark?

For starters, let's look at the Price to Earnings of the SP500 as a whole.

The median or average price-to-earnings ratio over the past hundred years has been about 15, meaning the value of the SP500 should be 15 times its current earnings.

Currently, we're at about 26 times earnings. Here's a table of the earnings history of the past 5 years. Each month reports the past year's earnings.

Date	Value	Date	Value
December 31, 2024	211.28	November 30, 2022	177.58
November 30, 2024	207.61	October 31, 2022	182.40
October 31, 2024	200.94	September 30, 2022	187.23
September 30, 2024	206.27	August 31, 2022	188.91
August 31, 2024	199.10	July 31, 2022	190.55
July 31, 2024	197.93	June 30, 2022	192.26
June 30, 2024	196.76	May 31, 2022	194.14
May 31, 2024	194.07	April 30, 2022	196.03
April 30, 2024	193.18	March 31, 2022	197.91
March 31, 2024	191.20	February 28, 2022	197.90
February 29, 2024	191.74	January 31, 2022	197.63
January 31, 2024	192.08	December 31, 2021	197.87
December 31, 2023	192.43	November 30, 2021	190.39
November 30, 2023	189.70	October 31, 2021	182.91
October 31, 2023	186.98	September 30, 2021	175.43
September 30, 2023	184.23	August 31, 2021	169.57
August 31, 2023	188.17	July 31, 2021	164.22
July 31, 2023	182.09	June 30, 2021	158.76
June 30, 2023	181.01	May 31, 2021	148.57
May 31, 2023	179.06	April 30, 2021	138.39
April 30, 2023	177.12	March 31, 2021	128.20
March 31, 2023	176.17	February 28, 2021	116.84
February 28, 2023	174.36	January 31, 2021	108.49
January 31, 2023	175.54	December 31, 2020	94.13
December 31, 2022	172.75	November 30, 2020	95.49

What we see here is that earnings have grown 120% over the last 5 years. That seems impressive at first glance. However, the starting point here is after a significant decline in earnings throughout 2020. Which took the earnings amount back to the same place as 2016, basically wiping out 4 years of growth.

Now why would the SP500 trade at 26 times earnings if the average has been 15?

The market is a forward-looking beast that is always about tomorrow and next year.

So if we look at forward earnings instead of current earnings, we get a good indication of why the market is where it is. The following table shows the price-to-earnings of the SP500 based on projected earnings till December 2026. What we see is that the current projection of earnings places today's market price at about 20 times earnings, which is equal to a 30% increase in earnings. (26/20=30%)

Date	Value	Date	Value
December 31, 2026	20.15	December 31, 2023	27.31
September 30, 2026	20.67	September 30, 2023	25.98
June 30, 2026	21.33	June 30, 2023	23.89
March 31, 2026	22.03	March 31, 2023	23.41
December 31, 2025	22.96	December 31, 2022	23.79
September 30, 2025	23.90	September 30, 2022	20.52
June 30, 2025	25.35	June 30, 2022	18.63
March 31, 2025	26.20	March 31, 2022	22.51
December 31, 2024	27.18	December 31, 2021	22.90
September 30, 2024	29.37	September 30, 2021	25.96
June 30, 2024	29.10	June 30, 2021	27.66
March 31, 2024	28.52	March 31, 2021	33.98

This is all great and very possible in normal times. However, if CEOs are restraining themselves from making big new investments due to the uncertain trade environment we are in, then all the projections are off. All this growth can only happen in a business-friendly country.

Furthermore, the SP500 has increasingly become reliant on international revenue. The question will be whether this revenue will be reliable as countries become less friendly towards the USA. As Mark Carney said yesterday, "The old relationship with the US is over."

S&P 500: Aggregate Geographic Revenue Exposure (%)
(Source: FactSet)

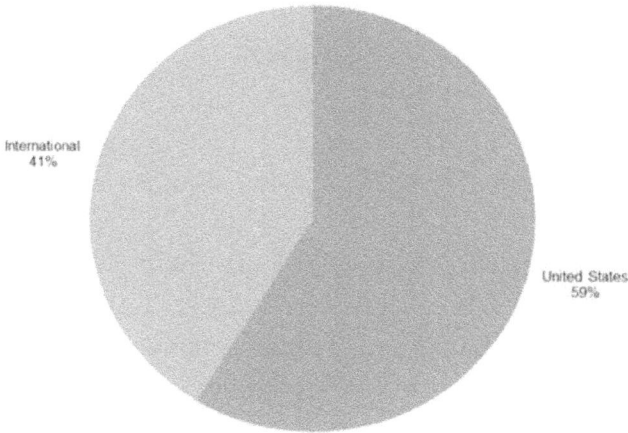

International
41%

United States
59%

With many countries feeling the US is an unreliable trade partner, we may be entering a time when the international earnings of the SP500 will diminish.

So what's the good news? What's the solution?

There will likely be a point sometime soon when Trump listens to the market and stops all the chaos. He will need to take ownership of the recent consumer confidence decline. At some point, his rhetoric will need to subside. In the meantime, we should be able to get good opportunities at a reasonable price in the next short while, after the next leg down.

DEALING WITH THE CERTAINTY OF UNCERTAINTY

April 4 2025

Someone just asked me if I'm nervous about the markets.

Many are comparing the current uncertainty to the economic uncertainty that existed in the early days of COVID. The only difference is that back then, people were genuinely concerned about their lives and the lives of their loved ones. Now, the uncertainty is purely economic.

The VIX, a measure of market volatility or a fear gauge of market participants, is up 45% today alone at the time of writing. And up more than 130% in the past ten days.

Markets are down 6% on the day! This seems like panic for many.

Many have said that tariffs will lead to a scenario similar to the Great Depression of the 1930s. They cite history as a testament to this predicament. You can read about that time in the Britannica.

Getting back to the question. Let me tell you three reasons why I'm not nervous.

Number one: The positions I'm taking for clients consist of solid, long-term companies that will not only weather this storm but also emerge unscathed and in better shape. There aren't any holdings I have recommended and purchased for clients that will suffer long-term from these trade negotiations.

Number two: I'm not buying into the notion that we're in this trade war for the long term. Instead, my understanding is that this is a form of negotiation, both the tariffs from the White House and the counter-tariffs from China and elsewhere. These negotiations may take three to six months or longer to play out, but my current thesis is that once they are resolved, the markets will begin climbing higher in short order. The markets won't even wait until everything is sorted out; they will start climbing in anticipation of fruitful negotiations.

Number three: This time is not comparable to the Great Depression at all. The FED has learned many lessons from the past. Jerome Powell, chair of the Federal Reserve, is extremely competent and has a very capable team working hard to decide which next move is correct. They understand the consequences of making mistakes and have established careful measures to shape their policy and make the right decisions, contrary to what politicians may claim.

That doesn't mean there won't be any businesses failing in the short term. There is a high likelihood that many small businesses will close in the next six months, especially those with significant debt that have been outsourcing their manufacturing to China. These small businesses may struggle to navigate the short-term cycle of negotiations.

Regarding the economy as a whole, yes, if this trade war were to continue, it would be devastating to the economy. However, that's unlikely to happen.

So, while a short-term recession is definitely in the works, a Great Depression scenario is not due anytime soon.

Should we be buying stocks at current prices?

So, where does that leave us? Should we be buying stocks at current prices? Is this a massive opportunity, or will there be more room to fall?

These are the questions I'm fielding.

The short term is challenging to predict—actually impossible to know—and that is the uncertainty investors need to deal with. However, the long term, let's say 18-24 months out, will be higher and better. And this we can say with certainty. The White House needs to be taken at face value. They have been following through with everything they have said. For better or for worse. They will definitely work hard to get these trade negotiations done correctly over the coming year or less.

It's nice to have certainty in life. Many people can't handle the lack of it. So, we need to shift our outlook from short-term to long-term to create certainty.

Nonetheless, we should strive to conduct some form of short-term analysis to the best of our ability. Otherwise, we'll miss out on promising opportunities.

Last week, I mentioned that we will likely move closer to the trend line that started in early COVID.

We have declined nearly 9% this week and are currently very close to the trend line mentioned. See the weekly bar chart below. The purple line represents the trend we are referencing. Currently, we stand about 3% above that line.

Does that mean we should buy everything we can once we reach the line? No. We need to take it easy here, as such technical analysis is not guaranteed to hold up against extreme volatility.

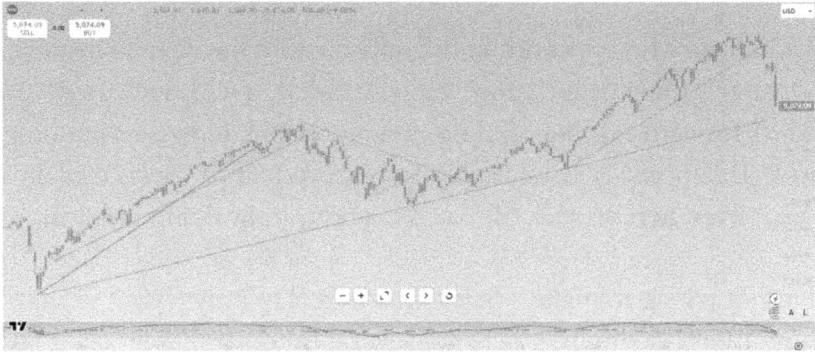

In fact, a major move like today indicates that this direction is likely to persist for at least another day or so. Additionally, the fact that the markets finished the day and week at the bottom of their trading pattern is a bearish sign.

For now, I believe we should wait to see how the market behaves over the next few days. There is a risk of missing the bottom, but sometimes we don't need to catch it. As they say during such times, "don't catch a falling knife." Let the knife land before picking it up.

Is there any action to take now?

This pertains to the market as a whole. However, certain holdings are being significantly undervalued, akin to 'throwing out the baby with the bathwater.' For instance, I am currently watching Aritzia (ATZ on the TSX). This stock has a promising future and is increasing its earnings in the high double digits. As it has pulled back from the low $70s to the $40 range, it appears to be a strong buy for clients who can manage short-term uncertainty.

I anticipate this opportunity to double within the next 24 months. Once the trade negotiations are concluded, it will trade at 20-25 times forward earnings and rise to around $85. However, jumping in at this point is not suitable for everyone. For most, it makes sense even here to wait till you see a bottom or rising pattern.

I'm not trying to make a prediction here. I'm only trying to share how I look at things. There are several other similar stocks I am thinking of along the same lines. Here, I'm sharing what's going through my mind at this moment.

Dollar Cost Averaging

Another approach is Dollar Cost Averaging, which involves committing a set amount to invest in new positions regularly. For instance, if we wanted to purchase $50,000 worth of Aritzia, we could spread this investment over the next few weeks or months, buying $10,000 at five different intervals to average our price amidst uncertainty.

Hopefully, that helps you in this time of uncertainty.

TAKEAWAY FROM THE LATEST TARIFF SAGA

May 12 2025

As this book is going to print now in mid-May 2025, we've had a whirlwind of a ride in the markets over the last few months, and there is a lot to unpack from this experience.

As we have news about the successful initial negotiations between China and US envoys who met in Switzerland over the weekend, a promising, rosy path ahead is beginning to take shape. Instead of the negative bashing, we now have a positive outlook again. As the markets are now jumping upwards over three percent on the day, it's a good time to reflect on some lessons from the past few months and gain clarity on where we currently stand market-wise.

Technical Analysis Focus

With all the tremendous uncertainty that we have had with markets dropping 20% in a short period of time, from the highs of late February to the lows of early April, it's fascinating to see that in hindsight, the technical charts were extremely predictable. I had been writing about this to my clients throughout the downturn, and I have shared some of my letters here.

First, let's take a big picture look with this daily candle chart of the S&P 500. We line up the bottoms of the market swings over the last five years since March 2020, the early COVID era, when the markets dropped about 35% in one month. This creates the upward-trending purple line spanning over five years.

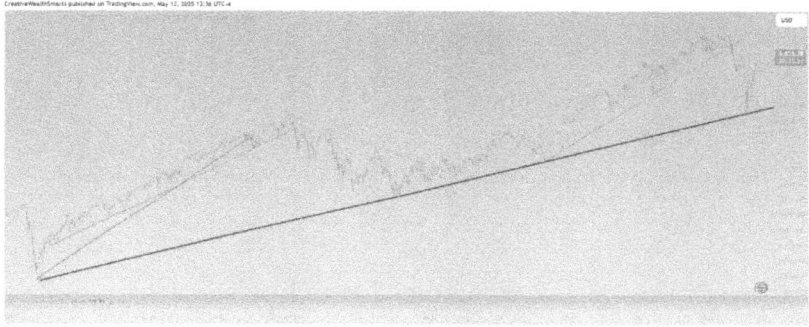

We can see that the last time we touched this trend line was in October 2023. Since that touch, we began a steeper incline that culminated in February 2025. We can follow this steep incline with the orange line, and we can observe how this line was violated in late February.

By zooming in on the next daily candle chart, we can see that once the orange trend line was breached, it made sense that we were heading down to the long-term purple trend line below. This purple trend line had been established and tested several times before. Sure enough, as soon as it reached the trend line, it bounced up and began a new upward rebound pattern.

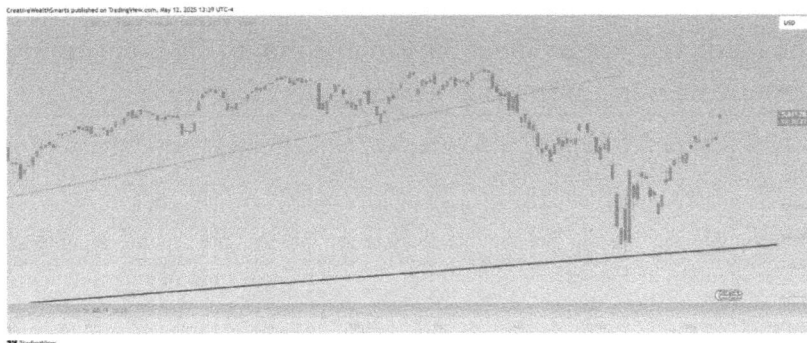

Although this may seem predictable in hindsight, the problem is that during the days when the market was crashing, from April 3rd to April 8th, it dropped so rapidly and with such overwhelming negative sentiment that the average investor was likely spooked and deterred from making a significant buy.

My clients who had cash available in high-interest savings and money market funds were advised that it was a good time to allocate 33-50% of that cash to the equity markets. But here's the thing: when there's such strong momentum driving the markets down, there's a high likelihood that the trendline may not hold. It looks like a tsunami that will overcome any barrier. This makes it extremely difficult to have high conviction at such a time when we were at the purple trendline. And that was precisely the best time to buy as markets hit a level last seen in January 2024, over 15 months prior.

> *"The time to buy is when there's blood in the streets."*
> – Baron Rothschild

If you play it safe and wait till all the stars are lined up in perfect formation, you are paying a much higher price, as Warren

Buffett warned: *"You pay a very high price in the stock market for a cheery consensus."*

Buy, Sell, or Hold?

So, here we are, as the markets have climbed 19% off their recent low, and the question is, what do you do now? Buy, Sell, or Hold?

For the US markets as a whole, there will be a lot of positivity as trade deals are woven over the coming months, so my advice is not to sell. Specific holdings that may be poised for a pullback need their own analysis and are a different story.

However, based on the two quotes above from Rothschild and Buffett, it's also not the ideal time to buy. Again, specific holdings are a different story, but the market as a whole is now in a positive consensus or "cheery consensus" as Buffett put it, which means you're paying an expensive price.

However, it's also difficult to be on the sidelines with cash when there is currently an optimistic view, and many would say "better late than never," which may apply here as well. So, as we are 5% off the recent February high, we should be looking for a pullback entry point.

So if you're buying now, just know you're paying a higher price. That means you should be more cautious in your purchases.

I suppose it's reasonable to be a cautious buyer at this time.